Cicero: In Catilinam I-IV

CICERO

IN CATILINAM I-IV

Edited with Introduction
and Notes by

J.F. Stout

Bristol Classical Press

This edition 2009
Bristol Classical Press
an imprint of
Gerald Duckworth & Co Ltd
90-93 Cowcross Street, London EC1M 6BF
Tel: 020 7490 7300
Fax: 020 7490 0080
info@duckworth-publishers.co.uk
www.ducknet.co.uk

First published by University Tutorial Press Ltd in 1911

A catalogue record for this book is available
from the British Library

ISBN 978 1 85399 719 8

Printed and bound in Great Britain by
CPI Antony Rowe, Chippenham and Eastbourne

CONTENTS.

PREFATORY NOTE

In this edition the notes on the first of the Speeches against Catiline were provided by T. T. Jeffery, M.A., and T. R. Mills, M.A., and the notes on the third Speech by A. W. Young. M.A., and W. F. Masom, M.A. These have been revised and the notes on the second and fourth Speeches written by J. F. Stout, M.A.

INTRODUCTION.

§ 1. **Marcus Tullius Cicero,** the greatest of Roman orators, was born near Arpinum in 106 B.C. His family was of equestrian rank, but had never held any office in Rome. Cicero was accordingly a *novus homo,* and his struggle to obtain the praetorship and consulship was on that account made harder. He was sent while still a young lad to Rome, and there studied under the best masters, such as Archias. In B.C. 91 he assumed the *toga virilis,* and then attended the lectures of orators and lawyers. He was entrusted by his father to the special care of Mucius Scaevola, the Augur, from whose side he hardly ever departed. At that time one of the easiest methods of obtaining fame and success was by means of oratory, and as Cicero had a natural talent for this art, he cultivated it in preference to devoting himself to a military life. However, he served, as was usual with young Romans who aspired to public office, one campaign, and this happened to be in the Social War (89 B.C.) under Cn. Pompeius Strabo (the father of Pompeius the Great). For the next six years he took no part in public affairs, but devoted his time to the study of rhetoric and the various schools of philosophy; from Phaedrus he learned the Epicurean system, from Philo that of the New Academy, and from Diodŏtus that of the Stoics.

The first of his extant speeches is that *Pro P. Quinctio,* which was delivered in 81 B.C. Next year, in a criminal trial, he defended Sextus Roscius Amerinus, whose accuser was Chrysogŏnus, the powerful freedman of Sulla. It was bold in Cicero to undertake this defence and thereby to risk the anger of Sulla, but his boldness was equalled by

C. CAT. I.-IV.   1

his eloquence, and his success on this occasion placed
him at once amongst the best orators of the day. Ill-
health obliged him to retire to Rhodes and Athens, where
he continued his study of rhetoric and philosophy for
two years, returned to Rome in 77 B.C., and was elected
quaestor for the year 75 B.C. He served this office at
Lilybaeum in Sicily, and acquired golden opinions from the
natives through his integrity, impartiality, and self-denial.
In 74 B.C. he returned to Rome, and again devoted himself
to his profession as an advocate. In 70 B.C. he undertook
the impeachment of Verres, who was charged by the
Sicilians with having been guilty of misgovernment, oppres-
sion, and extortion when propraetor in Sicily, 73–71 B.C.
Hortensius, the consul-elect for the following year, was
Verres' advocate, and on behalf of his client was anxious
that the trial should be delayed until the next year, when
the presiding Praetor would be more favourably disposed
to the defendant. Cicero frustrated this attempt by getting
his evidence ready in half the time allowed, and by opening
his case very briefly and proceeding at once to the examina-
tion of his witnesses. The result of Cicero's onslaught
was that Verres departed at once into exile without even
attempting a defence.

In politics Cicero was a fairly consistent member of the
Senatorial party, or party of the Nobles (*Optimātes*); the
opposition was the Democratic party, or party of the People,
and there were numbers of disappointed men of all ranks
of society ready for revolution in any form if they could find
a leader. Cicero was Curule Aedile 69 B.C., Praetor 66 B.C.
—in this year he advocated the *Lex Manilia*, giving to
Pompeius the conduct of the war against Mithradātes—and
Consul 63 B.C. The revolutionary movement had by this
time taken the form of a widespread conspiracy; its
members were of every class, even senators and consulars;
it had branches in many Italian towns; its object was to
overthrow the government of the Senate by violence and
substitute a Democratic government; and from the name
of its leader, it was known as the Catilinarian conspiracy.

Its first step was to be the assassination of Cicero; but the latter by means of spies kept himself informed of all its movements, and at the close of 63 B.C. suddenly arrested the leading conspirators. A few days later he had them executed (although as Roman citizens they were exempt from such punishment), and the remainder, attempting to carry out their plans by force of arms, were defeated at Pistoria, in Northern Etruria, where Catilina fell. The surviving conspirators fled to the provinces, and in particular to Greece. For his services on this occasion Cicero received extraordinary marks of honour, including the title of *Pater Patriae.*

In 60 B.C. the Democratic Party found leaders in Caesar, Pompeius (recently returned triumphant from the war in Asia), and Crassus; these formed the coalition known as the First Triumvirate. They determined to get rid of Cicero, who was too good an Optimate to please them; and they employed for the purpose P. Clodius, an unprincipled Democrat, and a Tribune of the year 58 B.C. Clodius drew attention to the illegality of the execution of the Catilinarians, overawed both Senate and Consuls by the violence of his attitude and the presence of his armed partisans, and ultimately compelled Cicero to go into banishment. In the next year Pompeius quarrelled with Clodius, and to spite him procured the recall of Cicero (57 B.C.), who, his political activity being crippled by the Triumvirate, devoted his eloquence to the defence of his friends. In 56 B.C. he delivered his speech *Pro Sestio,* in 54 B.C. the *Pro Plancio,* and in 52 B.C. the *Pro Milone.* In 55 B.C. he was admitted to the College of Augurs; and in 51 B.C. he acted as Governor of the province of Cilicia, where he conducted with success some small military operations.

About this time Pompeius came over from the side of Caesar to that of the Senate; and accordingly, when Caesar marched upon Rome 49 B.C., Cicero, after some hesitation, joined Pompeius; but subsequently, after the battle of Pharsalia in 48 B.C., he was reconciled to Caesar. After the death of Caesar, 44 B.C., an open rupture ensued between him and Antonius, and Cicero gave vent to his anger and indignation in the famous *Philippic Orations*, fourteen speeches, the finest and most renowned of which is the second. From the beginning of 43 B.C. until the end of April, Cicero was in the height of his glory, but before the end of that year, in the proscription that followed upon the formation of the Second Triumvirate, Cicero's name was, on the suggestion of Antonius, put in the list of those doomed to summary destruction. Soldiers were immediately sent in pursuit, and although his attendants wished to offer resistance, Cicero forbade them, and surrendered to his pursuers, by whom he was killed.

In the foregoing sketch no mention has been made of Cicero's numerous and important works on rhetoric and philosophy. His activity in this direction begins from his exile in 57 B.C.; in 55 B.C. he produced the *De Oratore*, in 54–51 B.C. the *De Re Publica*, and in 52 B.C. the *De Legibus*. This period of activity was followed by five years (51 to 46 B.C.) of comparative rest, but in 46 B.C. he wrote the *Hortensius* or *De Philosophia*, a treatise now lost, in addition to the *Partitiones Oratoriae*, the *Brutus* or *De Claris Oratoribus*, and the *Orator*. During the years 45 and 44 B.C. he wrote the *De Consolatione*, on the occasion of the death of his daughter Tullia; the *Academica*, an account of the new Academic Philosophy, which maintained that there was no such thing as certainty—we must be content with probability; the *Disputationes Tusculanae*, treating of happiness and morality; the *De Natura Deorum*, the *De Divinatione* (on the subject whether gods communicate with men by means of augury, etc.), the *Cato Maior* or *De Senectute*, the *De Amicitia*, the *De Fato* (an account of Fate and Freewill), the *Paradoxa* (an account of certain paradoxical opinions of the Stoics), the *De Officiis*, a treatise on duty, and the *De Finibus*, on the Highest Good.

So far we have dealt with Cicero's speeches and his rhetorical and philosophical works. We must also mention (1) his *Letters*, of which he wrote a vast number, and of which nearly 800 are preserved; (2) his *Poetical Works*, which were very poor in quality though not small in quantity—his chief poem was written on the subject of his consulship; and (3) his *Historical and Miscellaneous Works, e.g.* a prose account of his consulship, an account of his policy immediately previous to his consulship, etc.

§ 2. **Sketch of Roman History.**—From the first days of the Republic, when Rome was a small city with but a few square miles of territory, it was recognised as the main feature of the constitution that the government of the state should be jointly in the hands of people, magistrates, and Senate. The magistrates were on their election entrusted by the people with the task of carrying on the administration from year to year, and usually there was no interference with their jurisdiction; still the people was the ultimate source of power, and could make its will felt by passing laws when assembled in its comitia. The Senate's duty consisted in discussing such matters as were laid before it by the chief magistrates, and in giving advice about the course which seemed best under the circumstances, but it could not compel the magistrates to adopt any mode of action that was distasteful to them: it could only demand that its advice should not be dismissed without due consideration. When the territory of Rome expanded beyond its early narrow limits, and began to extend over Italy, the old theory of the constitution was lost sight of, and the Senate, which consisted for the most part of ex-magistrates, and so included many men of great experience in administration, assumed more and more power; for the people, besides being incompetent to decide on the spur of the moment difficult questions of home and foreign policy, could not often make the long journey to the capital, and the magistrates grew continually more averse to act in opposition to the experienced council of which they would one day themselves be members. Thus the Senate became supreme, and for many years it justified its usurped authority by the combined prudence and vigour of its action. By its energy and patriotism it carried the nation triumphantly through the dangerous struggle with Pyrrhus (280–275 B.C.), and the still more dangerous and exhausting conflict with Hannibal (218–202 B.C.), and the credit which these successes brought gave additional strength to its rule. In the fifty years which followed upon the second Punic war, and which are known as the " first period of foreign conquest," many brilliant victories were won, and the dominions of Rome spread far and wide outside Italy. Philip and Perseus of Macedonia were defeated respectively at Cynoscephalae (197 B.C.) and Pydna (168 B.C.) in the second and third Macedonian wars, and the empire that was once ruled by Alexander the Great sank into a province of Rome. Antiochus of Syria lost the battle of Magnesia to Scipio, the conqueror of Hannibal, and was deprived of one-half of his empire, 190 B.C. Greece was reduced to subjection after its great town Corinth had been taken and sacked, 146 B.C.; and in the same year Carthage, a still more powerful centre of commerce, was razed to the ground after a desperate resistance. During all these years scarce a whisper was heard against the Senate; and yet its period of greatness was over, and there only remained to it perpetual conflict with people, magistrates, and army. For the great conquests proved its ruin: in the first place, as the empire expanded, the Senate could no longer exercise efficient control over the generals and armies which it sent out to distant provinces; secondly, the senators themselves were not simple honest citizens, as they had been in earlier times, but were ready to enrich themselves by every unjust means at the expense of those whom they governed; and thirdly, in consequence of the great wealth that flowed to Rome from the conquered peoples, the farmers and labourers left the country districts and flocked to the capital to sell their votes and break out into riot if their demands were not gratified. In 133 B.C., when Tiberius Gracchus made the first attack upon the Government, there were some two thousand families, senatorial and equestrian, who grew rich by the plunder of the provincials, while the rest of the citizens were in a poverty from which there seemed no release. Tiberius fell, but the fight was continued by his brother Gaius (121 B.C.), Saturninus (100 B.C.), and other reformers as gallant and as ill-fated. The Senate resisted with the usual tenacity of an oligarchy: sometimes it lost ground, but never for long, and when the struggle had gone on for half a century, Sulla, its great champion, returned at the head of his victorious troops from a war against Mithradates of Pontus (87–84 B.C.). The constitution which he framed was a subversion of that early theory which has been mentioned above, for he placed the Senate in the real possession of the government by diminishing the powers of the magistrates—especially of the tribunes who had taken the chief part in the attack on the Senate—and he only allowed the people to pass laws in the comitia subject to restrictions. Such enactments were resented by the democrats—the party of the Gracchi and Saturninus: but in addition to this source of hostility, the confiscations and proscriptions of Sulla himself were the cause of lasting discontent. Throughout Italy, but especially in Etruria, he had ejected whole communities to make way for his veterans, though these old soldiers had little taste for the monotony of agricultural life, and longed for fresh campaigns. During the troubles of the Sullan dictatorship many nobles had lost and made fortunes; and they were willing to take part in any fresh rising that offered to relieve them from their debts and give them new wealth. Yet in spite of the discontent among democrats and the dispossessed, the Sullan constitution might have stood if the Senate could only have kept its generals and armies under control. As it was, militarism became rampant, and when in 70 B.C. Pompeius and Crassus, both returning from successful campaigns at the head of their troops, made an alliance with the democrats, and declared against the legislation of Sulla, the Senate had perforce to yield and to assent to its repeal. From this date Roman history becomes in an increasing degree the history of its generals; in 67 B.C. Pompeius by a vote of the people received the chief command against the pirates with almost monarchical powers; and this authority was continued to him in 66 B.C. for the purpose of crushing Mithradates, who was for a third time at war with Rome. The career of Pompeius in Asia was one of scarcely broken success, and almost every day brought news of fresh triumphs on his part. He defeated Mithradates, and compelled him to flee from his kingdom to the Tauric Chersonese (*Crimea*), received the abject submission of the hitherto victorious Tigranes of Armenia, and then, turning south, compelled Bedouins, Arabs, and Jews to submission, and extended the bounds of the empire as far as the Euphrates. These successes were not altogether gratifying to the Senate, for experience had shown how difficult it was to deal with a victorious general, but they were even more distasteful to the democrats, for they had no guarantee that they might not result in a tyranny as hateful as Sulla's. Crassus, the richest man in Rome, and the recognised chief of the bankers and money-lenders, had previously quarrelled with Pompeius and dreaded his return, and the feeling was naturally shared by Caesar and the other leaders of the democrats, among whom we must class Catilina.

§ 3. **History of the Catilinarian Conspiracies.**—While the senatorial party was on the whole united, at least in their efforts to preserve the *status quo*, the party grouped roughly under the title of *populares* was a heterogeneous one. Some of them were genuine reformers; others, led by Crassus, consisted of capitalists who saw that the feeble oligarchic administration was a menace to provincial trade; a very large number consisted of the discontented classes who had everything to gain and nothing to lose by revolution. This section, which may be described as the anarchist or revolutionary section, consisted of patrician debauchees, and of bankrupts whose only hope of salvation depended on the cancelling of debts. These extremists, if they seemed at all likely to be successful, would be backed by the idle city mob. At the head of this party was Lucius Sergius Catilina, a man whose remarkable mental and physical powers were misused in a career of profligacy and crime. He was a patrician and had been a partisan of Sulla.

By 68 B.C., the year of his praetorship, he had spent all his fortune, and while propraetor of the rich province of Africa (67 B.C.) he sought to rehabilitate himself by the merciless plunder of his provincials. But on his return to Rome he was at once indicted for extortion. Since he knew that his plunder would be spent in bribing the judges in order to secure an acquittal, he determined to become a candidate for the consulship of 65 B.C., in the hope that he would gain a still more lucrative province as proconsul. But no citizen under indictment could become a candidate for office, and the presiding magistrate accordingly refused to nominate Catilina. The consuls elected, P. Cornelius Sulla and P. Autronius Paetus, were unseated for bribery and expelled from the Senate; whereupon they joined Catilina and Gnaeus Piso in a plot to murder Cotta and Torquatus, the consuls who took their place, on Jan. 1st, 65 B.C., the day of their entering upon office. The conspirators were then to seize the consulship and massacre the oligarchs. The plot failed, but suspicion fell upon Piso, whom the Senate sent to Spain, thinking to get him out of their way. Catilina hoped that Piso would hold Spain for the revolutionists, but he was murdered there by the Spaniards in the middle of 64 B.C. Caesar and Crassus were said by the aristocrats to be implicated in this first conspiracy of Catilina, but the evidence for their complicity is very slender; moreover the policy of the Knights was opposed to revolution, and a plot in which Caesar was involved would hardly end in failure. On the other hand, Caesar would doubtless have taken full advantage of the plot if it had been successful.

At the consular elections of 65 B.C. Catilina was again excluded from the list of candidates, as his trial was not yet over; later in the year he procured his acquittal by means of bribery.

In 64 B.C. Catilina began to organise his " second conspiracy," and in the autumn of that year was accepted for
the first time as a candidate for the consulship, which he
proposed to use as a means to revolution, to the cancelling
of debts, and to the supremacy of himself and his partisans.
The other candidates were Cicero and C. Antonius Hybrida,
a bankrupt senatorian of weak character who had been
won over by the conspirators. Cicero, though a parvenu
(*novus homo*), was supported by the Senate, since he was
now definitely ranged on the side of the *optimates*; this
support, together with that of the Knights and the
suffrages of the country voters, secured his election; the
conspirators by means of bribery procured the return
of Antonius, but Cicero soon detached him from their
side by resigning to him the lucrative province of
Macedonia.

Catilina, foiled in his hopes of the consulship, hard
pressed by his creditors, and dreading the return of
Pompeius from the East, which would put an end to his
plans, determined in 63 B.C. to seize the consulship by
force, and to have recourse to open revolt if the attempt
should fail. With the latter object in view he organised
an army from the Sullan veterans and other malcontents
in Italy, and appointed a centurion of Sulla called Manlius
as its leader, and Faesulae in Etruria as its base of operations. The attempt to seize the consulship was thwarted
by the vigilance of the consul Cicero, who was kept well
posted as to the designs of the conspirators. The consular
elections were postponed to October 21st in consequence
of the defiant attitude of Catilina. On October 20th
Cicero induced the Senate further to postpone the elections
till the 28th, and to discuss on the 21st the position of
public affairs. Accordingly on the 21st he challenged
Catilina to clear himself, and was met with insolent
defiance. The Senate thereupon by the illegal *consultum
ultimum* (see § 5) gave dictatorial powers to the consuls,
and sent the praetors to raise troops in Italy. On the 28th
Cicero presided at the elections clad in armour and with a

bodyguard, thus preventing all attempts at intimidation, and the result was that Catilina was again defeated.

The issue of this attempt to storm the consulship must have been foreseen by Catilina, for on October 27th Manlius had openly taken up arms at Faesulae. Owing to the secret information brought to Cicero, the other centres of discontent were taken by surprise, and Antonius was commissioned by the Senate to take the field against the revolutionists. Cicero's chief object was now to force Catilina's hand and make him join his army before his plans were completed. He was only waiting for more evidence.

On the night of November 6th a meeting of the conspirators was held at the house of M. Porcius Laeca, and two Roman knights undertook to murder Cicero in his bed on the morning of November 8th. The plot miscarried, owing to the vigilance of Cicero's spies. Cicero could now drive Catilina to action. On November 8th Cicero told the story of the attempt on his life in the Senate (**First Oration against Catilina**), and though Catilina had the effrontery to listen to the orator's denunciations, he rushed out of the Senate-house in a rage and left the same night for Etruria. On the next day Cicero called a public meeting and in his **Second Oration against Catilina** calmed the anxiety of the citizens and justified his own conduct. The Senate now declared Catilina and Manlius to be public enemies, but as yet no measures were taken against Lentulus and the other conspirators who had been left to mature the plot in Rome. Lentulus, the leader, was slow and timid; Cethegus and others urged immediate action; and finally it was decided that on December 19th Rome should be fired and the oligarchs murdered. But no arrests were made, as Cicero still required corroborative evidence.

This evidence was soon provided. The Narbonese Gauls had long been suffering from heavy tribute, forced levies, and the exactions of money-lenders, and there was then in Rome an embassy of the Allobroges seeking some remedy for their grievances. Since they met with no redress from the Senate, they were tempted to join the conspiracy.

At the critical moment Cicero bought them over, and
induced them to secure documents inculpating the conspirators. In accordance with a preconcerted plan, they
were on December 2nd arrested by Cicero's orders just as
they were leaving the city with these documents in their
possession. Early on the morning of December 3rd Cicero
procured the arrest of the conspirators. Later in the day
they were examined before the Senate and confessed their
guilt on being confronted with the Allobroges and the
incriminating documents. By a decree of the Senate they
were handed over to the leading citizens for custody.
Popular feeling had now veered round to the side of the
Senate; and in the evening of the same day (December 3rd)
Cicero held a public meeting and in his **Third Oration
against Catilina** informed the people of the events of the
day and of the precautions which the Senate had taken.
On December 5th Cicero, hearing of a plot to rescue the
prisoners, again convened the Senate. A long and wordy
debate ensued as to the punishment to be pronounced on
the conspirators. Silanus, the consul-elect, gave it as his
opinion that the prisoners should at once be executed. As
a matter of fact all cases affecting the *caput* or political
and personal rights of a citizen could be tried only by the
people or their delegates (see § 5). Caesar pointed this
out, hinted at the consequences of illegal action on the
Senate's part, and pleaded for a milder sentence. This
speech had a great effect upon the senators, and an
adjournment was proposed. Cicero then, in his **Fourth
Oration against Catilina**, compared the views of Silanus
and Caesar, and clearly showed that he favoured the
opinion of the former. The scale was turned by the
uncompromising young tribune-elect M. Porcius Cato, who
vigorously supported the death penalty. The *sententia* of
Cato was put to the vote, and a large majority voted in
favour of it. The same night the five conspirators,
Lentulus, Cethegus, Gabinius, Statilius, and Ceparius,
were strangled in the Tullianum or dungeon of the state-
prison near the Capitol.

Catilina, on hearing of the fate of the conspirators, tried to escape with his army into Transalpine Gaul, but the passes of the Apennines were occupied by the praetor Metellus Celer, while Antonius pressed upon his rear. At length in January 62 B.C. he turned on Antonius at the foot of the Apennines near Pistoria (*Pistoja*). His troops were killed almost to a man, and he himself fell after fighting with desperate courage.

§ **4. Remarks on the Catilinarian Conspiracies.**—Our two main authorities for these conspiracies are the speeches of Cicero and the " Catilinarian Conspiracy " of Sallust. Cicero was prejudiced in favour of the *Optimates*; Sallust was a friend of Caesar and an ardent democrat; but in the main the two accounts agree as to the character and aims of Catilina. Much divergence of opinion has existed as to the character and importance of the plots. It is generally considered that the first conspiracy was organised by Caesar and Crassus on behalf of the whole democratic party; but all the evidence that can be adduced in favour of this view rests upon the partisan statements of aristocrats. Moreover, the improbability of either of these leaders being implicated in such a revolutionary and ill-organised conspiracy has been pointed out above (see p. 9). Some maintain that the second plot also was a revolutionary movement against the Senate on the part of the democrats as a whole. But this is very improbable in itself, and is not borne out by our two chief authorities. Both conspiracies were probably the work of the anarchist and bankrupt section of the democratic party, with the able but ruined patrician Catilina at its head. The chief results of the second plot were that it strengthened the Senate, cast discredit on the democratic party, and was the cause of Cicero's rise to political distinction. The plot was ill-organised and never really formidable; but Cicero, in order to secure his position as a politician and patriot, magnified its importance a hundred-fold, and at the same time contrived that the democratic leaders should be

suspected of having taken part in it. The people of Rome
were thus won over to the side of the oligarchy, and the
attempts of Caesar to gain a military power which would
counterbalance that of Pompeius and ultimately enable him
to become mas†er of the Roman state were for a time
frustrated.

§ 5. Illegality of the Execution of the Conspirators by
Order of the Senate.—By the *Lex Valeria* of 509 B.C. it
was provided that " no magistrate should put to death or
scourge a Roman citizen without allowing appeal to the
people "; and from this time no power except the *comitia
centuriata* could pronounce the death sentence within the
walls of Rome. In later times all the capital jurisdiction
of the people was delegated to *quaestiones* or commission
courts, and these never had the power of inflicting the
death penalty. But the *caput* or personality of a Roman
consisted not only of the right to live, but also of the rights
of citizenship and freedom. Hence when we hear of the
infliction of capital punishment during the last two centuries of the Republic, we must understand by it not the
death penalty, but a penalty, generally that of exile,
involving the loss of citizenship. Thus infliction of death
even by the popular assembly had by this time fallen into
abeyance. When the Senate, which was in theory a
purely consultative assembly, had usurped the adminis-
trative powers of the people and magistrates, it sought to
trench on their rights of jurisdiction. After the office of
dictator had become practically extinct, it claimed and
exercised the right, when a grave crisis occurred, of
declaring the State to be in danger, and entrusting the
magistrates with dictatorial powers by the decree called
the *senatus consultum ultimum*, the formula of which
was *operam dent* (sc. *magistratus, quibus imperium est*)
ne quid res publica detrimenti capiat. The legality of
this power was always called in question: its only possible
justification was the fact that it might on some occasions
prevent the destruction of the State. But the real

sovereignty lay always with the people. In 121 B.C. Gaius Gracchus as tribune passed a plebiscite providing that no " trial in which the personal privileges (*caput*) of a Roman were in jeopardy could be held without the consent of the people." After the passing of this plebiscite the illegality of the " ultimate decree " was established beyond question. Cicero maintains that, as the Senate had declared the condemned men to be public enemies (*hostes*), they were no longer *cives*, and were outside the pale of the Sempronian plebiscite: but he is simply begging the question, for the very point as to whether the Catilinarians were *hostes* or not could not be determined by the Senate at all, but only by the permanent courts, to which the people had delegated their jurisdiction.

§ 6.   Chronological Table.

B.C.

68. Catilina praetor.

67. Catilina propraetor of Africa.

66. Catilina is threatened with impeachment for extortion in Africa, and so prevented from becoming a candidate for the consulship. His plot to murder Cotta and Torquatus, the consuls for 65 B.C., on January 1st, 65 B.C., is frustrated and postponed.

65. February 5th.—The postponed plot to murder the consuls is again frustrated.

Catilina is again prevented, owing to the indictment for extortion, from becoming a candidate for the consulship. He procures his acquittal by bribery.

64. Catilina's first candidature for the consulship. Cicero is elected (owing to the support of the Optimates and Equites), with Antonius, a Catilinarian, as his colleague.

63. Cicero and Antonius consuls. Catilina's second candidature for the consulship. The elections for consulship are put off till October 21st.

October 20th.—Speech by Cicero in the Senate on the danger of the State.

October 21st.—The elections for the consulship are again postponed. Cicero denounces Catilina. Exceptional powers voted to the consuls by the Senate's *consultum ultimum.*

October 27th.—Manlius raises the standard of revolt at Faesulae, in Etruria.

October 28th.—The elections for the consulship are held. Cicero overawes the Catilinarians, and the senatorial candidates are returned.

November 1st.—Failure of Catilina's attack on Praeneste.

November 6th to 7th (night).—Meeting of conspirators in Laeca's house. Two knights undertake to murder Cicero.

November 7th.—Cicero is informed of the plot to murder him.

November 8th.—Failure of the attempt to murder Cicero.

Cicero summons the Senate, and denounces Catilina in the **First Catilinarian Oration.** Catilina leaves Rome for the camp of Manlius.

November 9th.—Cicero summons a public assembly (*contio*) and delivers the **Second Catilinarian Oration.**

December 2nd (night).—Arrest, by previous arrangement, of the Allobroges as they are leaving Rome with papers proving the conspiracy.

December 3rd.—The conspirators are arrested, tried before the Senate, and convicted through the evidence of the Allobroges and of their own letters.

December 3rd (evening).—Cicero communicates the facts of the day to the people in the **Third Catilinarian Oration.**

December 5th.—At a meeting of the Senate to decide upon the punishment of the conspirators Cicero delivers the **Fourth Catilinarian Oration.** Sentence of death is passed and the conspirators are executed.

62. January 5th.—Catilina is defeated and slain at Pistoria, in Etruria, by M. Petreius.

M. TULLI CICERONIS
IN CATILINAM ORATIO PRIMA
HABITA IN SENATU.

I.

You are beyond all bearing, Catilina; your villainy has been detected, and yet you openly appear in the Senate.

Quo usque tandem abutere, Catilina, patientia nostra ? quam diu etiam furor iste tuus nos eludet ? quem ad finem sese effrenata iactabit audacia ? Nihilne te nocturnum praesidium Palatii, nihil urbis vigiliae, nihil timor populi, nihil concursus bonorum omnium, nihil hic munitis- 5 simus habendi senatus locus, nihil horum ora vultusque moverunt ? Patere tua consilia non sentis ? constrictam iam horum omnium scientia teneri coniurationem tuam non vides ? Quid proxima, quid superiore nocte egeris, ubi fueris, quos convocaveris, quid consilii ceperis, quem 10 nostrum ignorare arbitraris ? 2. O tempora, o mores ! senatus haec intellegit, consul videt: hic tamen vivit. Vivit ? immo vero etiam in senatum venit, fit publici consilii particeps, notat et designat oculis ad caedem unum quemque nostrum.   15

Our ancestors put men to death for less than you have done, while we shirk our duty.

Nos autem, fortes viri, satis facere rei publicae videmur, si istius furorem ac tela vitemus. Ad mortem te, Catilina, duci iussu consulis iam pridem oportebat, in te conferri pestem, quam tu in nos machinaris. 3. An vero vir amplissimus P. Scipio, pontifex maximus, Ti. Gracchum, 20 mediocriter labefactantem statum rei publicae, privatus interfecit: Catilinam, orbem terrae caede atque incendiis vastare cupientem, nos consules perferemus ? Nam illa

nimis antiqua praetereo, quod C. Servilius Ahala Sp.
Maelium, novis rebus studentem, manu sua occidit. Fuit, 25
fuit ista quondam in hac re publica virtus, ut viri fortes
acrioribus suppliciis civem perniciosum quam acerbissimum
hostem coercerent. Habemus senatus consultum in te,
Catilina, vehemens et grave; non deest rei publicae consilium neque auctoritas huius ordinis: nos, nos, dico aperte, 30
consules desumus.

II.

*Men like C. Gracchus have been killed on the spot for treason; but
while you flourish in your wickedness we still delay to draw the sword.*

4. Decrevit quondam senatus, ut L. Opimius consul
videret, ne quid res publica detrimenti caperet: nox nulla
intercessit; interfectus est propter quasdam seditionum
suspiciones C. Gracchus, clarissimo patre, avo, maioribus,
occisus est cum liberis M. Fulvius consularis. Simili 5
senatus consulto C. Mario et L. Valerio consulibus est
permissa res publica; num unum diem postea L. Saturninum
tribunum pl. et C. Servilium praetorem mors ac rei publicae
poena remorata est? At vero nos vicesimam iam diem
patimur hebescere aciem horum auctoritatis. Habemus 10
enim huiusce modi senatus consultum, verum inclusum in
tabulis, tamquam in vagina reconditum, quo ex senatus
consulto confestim te interfectum esse, Catilina, convenit.
Vivis, et vivis non ad deponendam, sed ad confirmandam
audaciam. Cupio, patres conscripti, me esse clementem, 15
cupio in tantis rei publicae periculis me non dissolutum
videri, sed iam me ipse inertiae nequitiaeque condemno.

*Meanwhile you are gathering an army against Rome. But you are
watched, and your punishment is only reserved until all the world shall
recognise the justice of it.*

5. Castra sunt in Italia contra populum Romanum in
Etruriae faucibus collocata, crescit in dies singulos hostium
numerus, eorum autem castrorum imperatorem ducemque 20

hostium intra moenia atque adeo in senatu videtis intesti-
nam aliquam cotidie perniciem rei publicae molientem⹀ Si
te iam, Catilina, comprehendi, si interfici iussero, credo, erit
verendum mihi, ne non potius hoc omnes boni serius a me
quam quisquam crudelius factum esse dicat. Verum ego 25
hoc, quod iam pridem factum esse oportuit, certa de causa
nondum adducor ut faciam. Tum denique interficiere, cum
iam nemo tam improbus, tam perditus, tam tui similis
inveniri poterit, qui id non iure factum esse fateatur.
6. Quam diu quisquam erit, qui te defendere audeat, vives, 30
sed vives ita, ut vivis, multis meis et firmis praesidiis
obsessus, ne commovere te contra rem publicam possis.
Multorum te etiam oculi et aures non sentientem, sicut
adhuc fecerunt, speculabuntur atque custodient.

III.

*You must be aware from my words in the Senate that your plots are
known, and therefore have no chance of success.*

Etenim quid est, Catilina, quod iam amplius exspectes, si
neque nox tenebris obscurare coetus nefarios nec privata
domus parietibus continere voces coniurationis tuae potest ?
si illustrantur, si erumpunt omnia ? Muta iam istam
mentem, mihi crede: obliviscere caedis atque incendiorum. 5
Teneris undique; luce sunt clariora nobis tua consilia
omnia, quae iam mecum licet recognoscas. 7. Meministine
me ante diem XII Kalendas Novembres dicere in senatu,
fore in armis certo die, qui dies futurus esset ante diem
VI Kalendas Novembres, C. Manlium, audaciae satellitem 10
atque administrum tuae ? Num me fefellit, Catilina, non
modo res tanta, tam atrox tamque incredibilis, verum, id
quod multo magis est admirandum, dies ?

*Have you forgotten that I foretold and prevented your intended
massacre of the aristocracy, and your attempt upon Praeneste?*

Dixi ego idem in senatu, caedem te optimatium contulisse
in ante diem V Kalendas Novembres, tum cum multi 15

principes civitatis Roma non tam sui conservandi quam
tuorum consiliorum reprimendorum causa profugerunt.
Num infitiari potes te illo ipso die meis praesidiis, mea
diligentia circumclusum commovere te contra rem publicam
non potuisse, cum tu discessu ceterorum nostra tamen, qui 20
remansissemus, caede te contentum esse dicebas ? 8.
Quid ? cum te Praeneste Kalendis ipsis Novembribus occu-
paturum nocturno impetu esse confideres, sensistine illam
coloniam meo iussu meis praesidiis, custodiis, vigiliis esse
munitam ? Nihil agis, nihil moliris, nihil cogitas, quod non 25
ego non modo audiam, sed etiam videam planeque sentiam.

IV.

*Lastly, I here denounce you, Senator of Rome as you are, for the
ringleader in a plot to murder me.*

Recognosce tandem mecum noctem illam superiorem:
iam intelleges multo me vigilare acrius ad salutem quam te
ad perniciem rei publicae. Dico te priore nocte venisse
inter falcarios—non agam obscure—in M. Laecae domum;
convenisse eodem complures eiusdem amentiae scelerisque 5
socios. Num negare audes ? quid taces ? convincam, si
negas; video enim esse hic in senatu quosdam, qui tecum
una fuerunt.   9. O di immortales ! ubinam gentium sumus ?
in qua urbe vivimus ? quam rem publicam habemus ? Hic,
hic sunt in nostro numero, patres conscripti, in hoc orbis 10
terrae sanctissimo gravissimoque consilio, qui de nostro
omnium interitu, qui de huius urbis atque adeo de orbis
terrarum exitio cogitent. Hos ego video consul et de re
publica sententiam rogo, et quos ferro trucidari oportebat,
eos nondum voce vulnero.   15

*You met your associates at Laeca's house, and laid your plans.
But again I was forewarned and forearmed.*

Fuisti igitur apud Laecam illa nocte, Catilina; distribuisti
partes Italiae; statuisti quo quemque proficisci placeret,
delegisti quos Romae relinqueres, quos tecum educeres,

discripsisti urbis partes ad incendia, confirmasti te ipsum
iam esse exiturum, dixisti paulum tibi esse etiam nunc 20
morae, quod ego viverem. Reperti sunt duo equites
Romani, qui te ista cura liberarent et sese illa ipsa nocte
paulo ante lucem me in meo lectulo interfecturos esse
pollicerentur. 10. Haec ego omnia, vixdum etiam coetu
vestro dimisso, comperi, domum meam maioribus praesidiis 25
munivi atque firmavi, exclusi eos, quos tu ad me salutatum
mane miseras, cum illi ipsi venissent, quos ego iam multis ac
summis viris ad me id temporis venturos esse praedixeram.

V.

*You must leave Rome. Providence has watched over us till now, but
we must take no more risks.*

Quae cum ita sint, Catilina, perge quo coepisti, egredere
aliquando ex urbe; patent portae: proficiscere. Nimium
diu te imperatorem tua illa Manliana castra desiderant.
Educ tecum etiam omnes tuos, si minus, quam plurimos;
purga urbem. Magno me metu liberabis, dum modo inter 5
me atque te murus intersit. Nobiscum versari iam diutius
non potes: non feram, non patiar, non sinam. 11. Magna
dis immortalibus habenda est atque huic ipsi Iovi Statori,
antiquissimo custodi huius urbis, gratia, quod hanc tam
taetram, tam horribilem tamque infestam rei publicae 10
pestem totiens iam effugimus. Non est saepius in uno
homine summa salus periclitanda rei publicae.

*So long as you attacked me only, I resisted you single-handed; now
you are attacking Rome and all Italy.*

Quam diu mihi, consuli designato, Catilina, insidiatus es,
non publico me praesidio, sed privata diligentia defendi.
Cum proximis comitiis consularibus me consulem in campo 15
et competitores tuos interficere voluisti, compressi conatus
tuos nefarios amicorum praesidio et copiis, nullo tumultu
publice concitato; denique, quotienscumque me petisti, per
me tibi obstiti, quamquam videbam perniciem meam cum

magna calamitate rei publicae esse coniunctam. 1. iam aperte rem publicam universam petis; templa c immortalium, tecta urbis, vitam omnium civium, It totam ad exitium et vastitatem vocas.

But I will not kill you, for that would not rid us of your followers. No; leave the city and take them with you.

Quare quoniam id, quod est primum et quod huius imperii disciplinaeque maiorum proprium est, facere nondum audeo, faciam id, quod est ad severitatem lenius, ad communem salutem utilius. Nam si te interfici iussero, residebit in re publica reliqua coniuratorum manus: sin tu, quod te iam dudum hortor, exieris, exhaurietur ex urbe tuorum comitum magna et perniciosa sentina rei publicae. 13. Quid est, Catilina? num dubitas id me imperante facere, quod iam tua sponte faciebas? Exire ex urbe iubet consul hostem. Interrogas me: num in exsilium? non iubeo, sed, si me consulis, suadeo.

VI.

You cannot wish to live among those who know and abhor your foul crimes.

Quid est enim, Catilina, quod te iam in hac urbe delectare possit? in qua nemo est extra istam coniurationem perditorum hominum, qui te non metuat, nemo, qui non oderit. Quae nota domesticae turpitudinis non inusta vitae tuae est? quod privatarum rerum dedecus non haeret in fama? quae libido ab oculis, quod facinus a manibus umquam tuis, quod flagitium a toto corpore afuit? cui tu adulescentulo, quem corruptelarum illecebris irretisses, non aut ad audaciam ferrum aut ad libidinem facem praetulisti? 14. Quid vero? nuper, cum morte superioris uxoris novis nuptiis domum vacuefecisses, nonne etiam alio incredibili scelere hoc scelus cumulasti? quod ego praetermitto et facile patior sileri, ne in hac civitate tanti facinoris immanitas aut exstitisse aut non vindicata esse videatur.

Even now ruin stares you in the face, and everywhere you are known for a traitor to your country.

Praetermitto ruinas fortunarum tuarum, quas omnes 15 proximus Idibus tibi impendere senties: ad illa venio, quae non ad privatam ignominiam vitiorum tuorum, non ad domesticam tuam difficultatem ac turpitudinem, sed ad summam rem publicam atque ad omnium nostrum vitam salutemque pertinent. 15. Potestne tibi haec lux, Catilina, 20 aut huius caeli spiritus esse iucundus, cum scias esse horum neminem qui nesciat, te pridie Kalendas Ianuarias Lepido et Tullo consulibus stetisse in comitio cum telo ? manum consulum et principum civitatis interficiendorum causa paravisse ? sceleri ac furori tuo non mentem aliquam aut 25 timorem tuum, sed fortunam populi Romani obstitisse ?

Your repeated attempts upon my life have all been in vain.

Ac iam illa omitto—neque enim sunt aut obscura aut non multa commissa postea—: quotiens tu me designatum, quotiens vero consulem interficere conatus es ! quot ego tuas petitiones ita coniectas, ut vitari posse non viderentur, 30 parva quadam declinatione et, ut aiunt, corpore effugi ! Nihil agis, nihil adsequeris, nihil moliris, neque tamen conari ac velle desistis. 16. Quotiens tibi iam extorta est ista sica de manibus ! quotiens excidit casu aliquo et elapsa est ! quae quidem quibus abs te initiata sacris ac devota sit, 35 nescio, quod eam necesse putas esse in consulis corpore defigere.

VII.

What can life in Rome be worth to you now?   Look at those empty benches round you and judge from them what loathing you now inspire in us.

Nunc vero quae tua est ista vita ?   Sic enim iam tecum loquar, non ut odio permotus esse videar, quo debeo, sed ut misericordia, quae tibi nulla debetur.   Venisti paulo ante in senatum.   Quis te ex hac tanta frequentia, tot ex tuis amicis ac necessariis salutavit ?   Si hoc post hominum 5 memoriam contigit nemini, vocis exspectas contumeliam, cum sis gravissimo iudicio taciturnitatis oppressus ? Quid, quod adventu tuo ista subsellia vacuefacta sunt, quod omnes consulares, qui tibi persaepe ad caedem constituti fuerunt, simul atque adsedisti, partem istam subselliorum nudam 10 atque inanem reliquerunt, quo tandem animo hoc tibi ferendum putas ?

Were I in your place I could not have stayed to endure such hatred and such dread.

17. Servi mehercule mei si me isto pacto metuerent, ut te metuunt omnes cives tui, domum meam relinquendam putarem: tu tibi urbem non arbitraris ? et si me meis 15 civibus iniuria suspectum tam graviter atque offensum viderem, carere me adspectu civium quam infestis omnium oculis conspici mallem: tu cum conscientia scelerum tuorum agnoscas odium omnium iustum et iam diu tibi debitum, dubitas, quorum mentes sensusque vulneras, 20 eorum adspectum praesentiamque vitare ?

And will you not heed even the voice of the State, our common mother, who now fears you and bids you begone?

Si te parentes timerent atque odissent tui neque eos ulla ratione placare posses, ut opinor, ab eorum oculis aliquo concederes: nunc te patria, quae communis est parens omnium nostrum, odit ac metuit et iam diu nihil te iudicat 25 nisi de parricidio suo cogitare: huius tu neque auctoritatem verebere nec iudicium sequere nec vim pertimesces ? 18. Quae tecum, Catilina, sic agit et quodam modo tacita loquitur: "Nullum iam aliquot annis facinus exstitit nisi per te, nullum flagitium sine te; tibi uni multorum civium 30 neces, tibi vexatio direptioque sociorum impunita fuit ac libera; tu non solum ad neglegendas leges et quaestiones, verum etiam ad evertendas perfringendasque valuisti. Superiora illa, quamquam ferenda non fuerunt, tamen, ut potui, tuli: nunc vero me totam esse in metu propter unum 35 te, quidquid increpuerit Catilinam timeri, nullum videri contra me consilium iniri posse, quod a tuo scelere abhorreat,

non est ferendum. Quam ob rem discede atque hunc mihi
timorem eripe, si est verus, ne opprimar, sin falsus, ut
tandem aliquando timere desinam.''
40

VIII.

*You stand self-condemned by your own offers to place yourself under
restraint.*

19. Haec si tecum ita ut dixi patria loquatur, nonne
impetrare debeat, etiam si vim adhibere non possit? Quid,
quod tu te ipse in custodiam dedisti? quod vitandae suspi-
cionis causa ad M'. Lepidum te habitare velle dixisti? a quo
non receptus etiam ad me venire ausus es atque ut domi 5
meae te adservarem rogasti. Cum a me quoque id responsum tulisses, me nullo modo posse isdem parietibus tuto
esse tecum, qui magno in periculo essem, quod isdem moenibus contineremur, ad Q. Metellum praetorem venisti: a
quo repudiatus ad sodalem tuum, virum optimum, M. 10
Metellum demigrasti, quem tu videlicet et ad custodiendum
diligentissimum et ad suspicandum sagacissimum et ad
vindicandum fortissimum fore putasti. Sed quam longe
videtur a carcere atque a vinculis abesse debere, qui se ipse
iam dignum custodia iudicarit? 15

*You challenge me to take a vote of the Senate. There is no need.
When I bid you go into exile, their silence gives consent.*

20. Quae cum ita sint, Catilina, dubitas, si emori aequo
animo non potes, abire in aliquas terras et vitam istam,
multis suppliciis iustis debitisque ereptam, fugae solitudi-
nique mandare? "Refer" inquis "ad senatum"; id enim
postulas et, si hic ordo placere decreverit te ire in exsilium, 20
obtemperaturum te esse dicis. Non referam, id quod
abhorret a meis moribus, et tamen faciam ut intellegas, quid
hi de te sentiant. Egredere ex urbe, Catilina, libera rem
publicam metu, in exsilium, si hanc vocem exspectas, proficiscere. Quid est, Catilina? ecquid attendis, ecquid 25
animadvertis horum silentium? Patiuntur, tacent. Quid

exspectas auctoritatem loquentium, quorum voluntatem
tacitorum perspicis ?

*Of no other man would they suffer me to speak thus; and outside the
Senate are Roman knights and citizens who now seek your death.*

21. At si hoc idem huic adulescenti optimo, P. Sestio,
si fortissimo viro, M. Marcello, dixissem, iam mihi consuli 30
hoc ipso in templo senatus iure optimo vim et manus
intulisset. De te autem, Catilina, cum quiescunt, probant,
cum patiuntur, decernunt, cum tacent, clamant; neque hi
solum, quorum tibi auctoritas est videlicet cara, vita
vilissima, sed etiam illi equites Romani, honestissimi atque 35
optimi viri, ceterique fortissimi cives, qui circumstant
senatum, quorum tu et frequentiam videre et studia
perspicere et voces paulo ante exaudire potuisti. Quorum
ego vix abs te iam diu manus ac tela contineo, eosdem
facile adducam, ut te haec, quae vastare iam pridem studes, 40
relinquentem usque ad portas prosequantur.

IX.

*But of exile I speak in vain; for I feel that no fear or shame can
move you.*

22. Quamquam quid loquor ? te ut ulla res frangat ? tu
ut umquam te corrigas ? tu ut ullam fugam meditere ? tu
ut ullum exsilium cogites ? Utinam tibi istam mentem di
immortales duint ! tametsi video, si mea voce perterritus
ire in exsilium animum induxeris, quanta tempestas in- 5
vidiae nobis, si minus in praesens tempus, recenti memoria
scelerum tuorum, at in posteritatem impendeat. Sed est
tanti, dum modo ista sit privata calamitas et a rei publicae
periculis seiungatur. Sed tu ut vitiis tuis commoveare, ut
legum poenas pertimescas, ut temporibus rei publicae cedas, 10
non est postulandum; neque enim is es, Catilina, ut te aut
pudor umquam a turpitudine aut metus a periculo aut ratio
a furore revocarit.

Go then, and join Manlius. In that camp of robbers you will be amongst your own people.

23. Quam ob rem, ut saepe iam dixi, proficiscere ac, si mihi inimico, ut praedicas, tuo conflare vis invidiam, recta 15 perge in exsilium: vix feram sermones hominum, si id feceris; vix molem istius invidiae, si in exsilium iussu consulis ieris, sustinebo. Sin autem servire meae laudi et gloriae mavis, egredere cum importuna sceleratorum manu, confer te ad Manlium, concita perditos cives, secerne 20 te a bonis, infer patriae bellum, exsulta impio latrocinio, ut a me non eiectus ad alienos, sed invitatus ad tuos isse videaris.

Go, as you have planned ; for I know that your silver eagle has already gone before you.

24. Quamquam quid ego te invitem, a quo iam sciam esse praemissos, qui tibi ad Forum Aurelium praesto- 25 larentur armati ? cui sciam pactam et constitutam cum Manlio diem ? a quo etiam aquilam illam argenteam, quam tibi ac tuis omnibus confido perniciosam ac funestam futuram, cui domi tuae sacrarium scelerum constitutum fuit, sciam esse praemissam ? Tu ut illa carere diutius 30 possis, quam venerari ad caedem proficiscens solebas, a cuius altaribus saepe istam impiam dexteram ad necem civium transtulisti ?

X.

Already your feet are firmly set upon the downward path, and you must pursue it to the end.

25. Ibis tandem aliquando, quo te iam pridem ista tua cupiditas effrenata ac furiosa rapiebat; neque enim tibi haec res adfert dolorem, sed quandam incredibilem volup- tatem. Ad hanc te amentiam natura peperit, voluntas exercuit, fortuna servavit. Numquam tu non modo otium, 5 sed ne bellum quidem nisi nefarium concupisti. Nactus es ex perditis atque ab omni non modo fortuna, verum etiam spe derelictis conflatam improborum manum.

Go, and bask in the admiration of those who will praise your evil lusts and your boasted strength, leaving me to thank Heaven that at least I have saved Rome from making you a consul.

26. Hic tu qua laetitia perfruere ! quibus gaudiis exsultabis ! quanta in voluptate bacchabere, cum in tanto 10 numero tuorum neque audies virum bonum quemquam neque videbis. Ad huius vitae studium meditati illi sunt qui ferentur labores tui, iacere humi non solum ad obsidendum stuprum, verum etiam ad facinus obeundum, vigilare non solum insidiantem somno maritorum, verum etiam 15 bonis otiosorum. Habes, ubi ostentes tuam illam praeclaram patientiam famis, frigoris, inopiae rerum omnium, quibus te brevi tempore confectum esse senties. 27. Tantum profeci tum, cum te a consulatu reppuli, ut exsul potius temptare quam consul vexare rem publicam posses, 20 atque ut id, quod esset a te scelerate susceptum, latrocinium potius quam bellum nominaretur.

XI.

I well know, gentlemen, that I may be asked why I thus suffer one convicted of treason to slip through my hands.

Nunc ut a me, patres conscripti, quandam prope iustam patriae querimoniam detester ac deprecer, percipite, quaeso, diligenter quae dicam, et ea penitus animis vestris mentibusque mandate. Etenim si mecum patria, quae mihi vita mea multo est carior, si cuncta Italia, si omnis res publica 5 sic loquatur: " M. Tulli, quid agis ? tune eum, quem esse hostem comperisti, quem ducem belli futurum vides, quem exspectari imperatorem in castris hostium sentis, auctorem sceleris, principem coniurationis, evocatorem servorum et civium perditorum, exire patiere, ut abs te non emissus ex 10 urbe, sed immissus in urbem esse videatur ? Nonne hunc in vincla duci, non ad mortem rapi, non summo supplicio mactari imperabis ?

*" Why do you hesitate ? " I hear it said ; " Is there no precedent for a
traitor's execution ? Surely by this you would earn the gratitude of
posterity, and have far less to fear than if you suffer him to spread death
and destruction through Italy."*

28. Quid tandem te impedit ? Mosne maiorum ? At
persaepe etiam privati in hac re publica perniciosos cives 15
morte multarunt. An leges, quae de civium Romanorum
supplicio rogatae sunt ? At numquam in hac urbe, qui a
re publica defecerunt, civium iura tenuerunt. An invidiam
posteritatis times ? Praeclaram vero populo Romano
refers gratiam, qui te, hominem per te cognitum, nulla 20
commendatione maiorum tam mature ad summum imperium per omnes honorum gradus extulit, si propter
invidiae aut alicuius periculi metum salutem civium tuorum
neglegis. 29. Sed si quis est invidiae metus, non est vehementius severitatis ac fortitudinis invidia quam inertiae ac 25
nequitiae pertimescenda. An cum bello vastabitur Italia,
vexabuntur urbes, tecta ardebunt, tum te non existimas
invidiae incendio conflagraturum ? "

XII.

*To this I answer that it was no fear of consequences to myself that
stayed my hand.*

His ego sanctissimis rei publicae vocibus et eorum hominum, qui hoc idem sentiunt, mentibus pauca respondebo.
Ego, si hoc optimum factu iudicarem, patres conscripti,
Catilinam morte multari, unius usuram horae gladiatori isti
ad vivendum non dedissem. Etenim si summi viri et 5
clarissimi cives Saturnini et Gracchorum et Flacci et superi-
orum complurium sanguine non modo se non contaminarunt,
sed etiam honestarunt, certe verendum mihi non erat, ne
quid hoc parricida civium interfecto invidiae in posteritatem
redundaret. Quodsi ea mihi maxime inpenderet, tamen 10
hoc animo fui semper, ut invidiam virtute partam gloriam,
non invidiam putarem.

*Catilina's death would have meant but a brief respite; but when he
has left Rome and taken his ruffians with him we shall have an acknowledged enemy in the field, but no traitors within our walls.*

30. Quamquam nonnulli sunt in hoc ordine, qui aut ea
quae imminent non videant, aut ea quae vident dissimulent,
qui spem Catilinae mollibus sententiis aluerunt coniura- 15
tionemque nascentem non credendo corroboraverunt:
quorum auctoritate multi, non solum improbi, verum
etiam imperiti, si in hunc animadvertissem, crudeliter et
regie factum esse dicerent. Nunc intellego, si iste, quo
intendit, in Manliana castra pervenerit, neminem tam 20
stultum fore, qui non videat coniurationem esse factam,
neminem tam improbum, qui non fateatur. Hoc autem
uno interfecto intellego hanc rei publicae pestem paulisper
reprimi, non in perpetuum comprimi posse. Quodsi se
eiecerit secumque suos eduxerit et eodem ceteros undique 25
collectos naufragos adgregarit, exstinguetur atque delebitur
non modo haec tam adulta rei publicae pestis, verum etiam
stirps ac semen malorum omnium.

XIII.

*The disease of violence and revolt has laid hold upon the body of the
State, and the death of one man would be a useless palliative.*

31. Etenim iam diu, patres conscripti, in his periculis
coniurationis insidiisque versamur, sed nescio quo pacto
omnium scelerum ac veteris furoris et audaciae maturitas
in nostri consulatus tempus erupit. Quodsi ex tanto latrocinio iste unus tolletur, videbimur fortasse ad breve quod- 5
dam tempus cura et metu esse relevati, periculum autem
residebit et erit inclusum penitus in venis atque in visceribus
rei publicae. Ut saepe homines aegri morbo gravi, cum
aestu febrique iactantur, si aquam gelidam biberunt, primo
relevari videntur, deinde multo gravius vehementiusque 10
adflictantur, sic hic morbus, qui est in re publica, relevatus
istius poena, vehementius reliquis vivis ingravescet.

Let us rather cast forth these men from our midst, and then they shall be crushed.

32. Quare secedant improbi, secernant se a bonis, unum in locum congregentur, muro denique, quod saepe iam dixi, secernantur a nobis; desinant insidiari domi suae consuli, 15 circumstare tribunal praetoris urbani, obsidere cum gladiis curiam, malleolos et faces ad inflammandam urbem comparare: sit denique inscriptum in fronte unius cuiusque, quid de re publica sentiat. Polliceor hoc vobis, patres conscripti, tantam in nobis consulibus fore diligentiam, 20 tantam in vobis auctoritatem, tantam in equitibus Romanis virtutem, tantam in omnibus bonis consensionem, ut Catilinae profectione omnia patefacta illustrata oppressa vindicata esse videatis.

Away, then, Catilina, with Rome's curse upon your head.   Now to thee, Jupiter, we pray for protection and for justice.

33. Hisce omnibus, Catilina, cum summa rei publicae 25 salute, cum tua peste ac pernicie cumque eorum exitio, qui se tecum omni scelere parricidioque iunxerunt, proficiscere ad impium bellum ac nefarium. Tu, Iuppiter, qui isdem quibus haec urbs auspiciis a Romulo es constitutus, quem Statorem huius urbis atque imperii vere nominamus, hunc 30 et huius socios a tuis ceterisque templis, a tectis urbis ac moenibus, a vita fortunisque civium omnium arcebis, et homines bonorum inimicos, hostes patriae, latrones Italiae, scelerum foedere inter se ac nefaria societate coniunctos, aeternis suppliciis vivos mortuosque mactabis.   35

M. TULLI CICERONIS
IN CATILINAM ORATIO SECUNDA
HABITA AD POPULUM.

I.

*Our first victory is won.   We have forced Catilina to declare himself
an open enemy.*

Tandem aliquando, Quirites, L. Catilinam, furentem
audacia, scelus anhelantem, pestem patriae nefarie molien-
tem, vobis atque huic urbi ferro flammaque minitantem,
ex urbe vel eiecimus vel emisimus vel ipsum egredientem
verbis prosecuti sumus. Abiit excessit, evasit erupit. 5
Nulla iam pernicies a monstro illo atque prodigio moenibus
ipsis intra moenia comparabitur. Atque hunc quidem
unum huius belli domestici ducem sine controversia vicimus.
Non enim iam inter latera nostra sica illa versabitur; non
in campo, non in foro, non in curia, non denique intra 10
domesticos parietes pertimescemus. Loco ille motus est,
cum est ex urbe depulsus. Palam iam cum hoste nullo
impediente bellum iustum geremus. Sine dubio perdidimus
hominem magnificeque vicimus, cum illum ex occultis
insidiis in apertum latrocinium coniecimus. 15

*He now knows himself baffled as he looks back at the city he has tried
in vain to bring to ruin.*

2. Quod vero non cruentum mucronem, ut voluit, extulit,
quod vivis nobis egressus est, quod ei ferrum e manibus
extorsimus, quod incolumes cives, quod stantem urbem
reliquit, quanto tandem illum maerore esse adflictum et
profligatum putatis ? Iacet ille nunc prostratus, Quirites, 20
et se perculsum atque abiectum esse sentit, et retorquet
oculos profecto saepe ad hanc urbem, quam e suis faucibus

32

creptam esse luget: quae quidem mihi laetari videtur,
quod tantam pestem evomuerit forasque proiecerit.

II.

*You may ask why I did not arrest him and put him to death. But
this would have aroused a storm of protest.*

3. Ac si quis est talis, quales esse omnes oportebat, qui
in hoc ipso, in quo exsultat et triumphat oratio mea, me
vehementer accuset, quod tam capitalem hostem non comprehenderim potius quam emiserim, non est ista mea culpa,
Quirites, sed temporum. Interfectum esse L. Catilinam et 5
gravissimo supplicio adfectum iam pridem oportebat, idque
a me et mos maiorum et huius imperii severitas et res
publica postulabat. Sed quam multos fuisse putatis, qui
quae ego deferrem non crederent, [quam multos, qui
propter stultitiam non putarent,] quam multos, qui etiam 10
defenderent, [quam multos, qui propter improbitatem
faverent] ? Ac si illo sublato depelli a vobis omne periculum iudicarem, iam pridem ego L. Catilinam non modo
invidiae meae, verum etiam vitae periculo sustulissem.

*And so I should have been hampered in taking action against the other
conspirators. I was obliged, therefore, to make him declare himself.
Once he is outside Rome I do not fear him or his followers.*

4. Sed cum viderem, ne vobis quidem omnibus re etiam 15
tum probata, si illum, ut erat meritus, morte multassem, fore
ut eius socios invidia oppressus persequi non possem, rem
huc deduxi, ut tum palam pugnare possetis, cum hostem
aperte videretis. Quem quidem ego hostem, Quirites,
quam vehementer foris esse timendum putem, licet hinc 20
intellegatis, quod etiam illud moleste fero, quod ex urbe
parum comitatus exierit. Utinam ille omnes secum suas
copias eduxisset ! Tongilium mihi eduxit, quem amare in
praetexta coeperat, Publicium et Minucium, quorum aes
alienum contractum in popina nullum rei publicae motum 25
adferre poterat: reliquit quos viros ! quanto aere alieno,
quam valentes, quam nobiles !

III.

Our armies can deal with his band of bankrupts and swindlers; it is the conspirators of high rank, whom he has left behind, that we have now to fear.   They are the more dangerous now that their designs are known.

5. Itaque ego illum exercitum prae Gallicanis legionibus et hoc dilectu, quem in agro Piceno et Gallico Q. Metellus habuit, et his copiis, quae a nobis cotidie comparantur, magno opere contemno, collectum ex senibus desperatis, ex agresti luxuria, ex rusticis decoctoribus, 5 ex iis, qui vadimonia deserere quam illum exercitum maluerunt; quibus ego non modo si aciem exercitus nostri, verum etiam si edictum praetoris ostendero, concident. Hos, quos video volitare in foro, quos stare ad curiam, quos etiam in senatum venire, qui nitent unguentis, qui 10 fulgent purpura, mallem secum suos milites eduxisset: qui si hic permanent, mementote non tam exercitum illum esse nobis quam hos, qui exercitum deseruerunt, pertimescendos. Atque hoc etiam sunt timendi magis, quod quid cogitent me scire sentiunt, neque tamen permoventur.   6. Video, cui 15 sit Apulia attributa, quis habeat Etruriam, quis agrum Picenum, quis Gallicum, quis sibi has urbanas insidias caedis atque incendiorum depoposcerit; omnia superioris noctis consilia ad me perlata esse sentiunt; patefeci in senatu hesterno die; Catilina ipse pertimuit, profugit: hi 20 quid exspectant ?   Ne illi vehementer errant, si illam meam pristinam lenitatem perpetuam sperant futuram.

IV.

They can expect little mercy from me, but I give them one more chance; let them join their leader.

Quod exspectavi, iam sum adsecutus, ut vos omnes factam esse aperte coniurationem contra rem publicam videretis: nisi vero si quis est, qui Catilinae similes cum Catilina sentire non putet.   Non est iam lenitati locus; severitatem res ipsa flagitat.   Unum etiam nunc concedam: 5 exeant, proficiscantur, ne patiantur desiderio sui Catilinam

miserum tabescere. Demonstrabo iter: Aurelia via profectus est; si accelerare volent, ad vesperam consequentur.

*Rome will be made the cleaner by their departure, as it has already
been by the expulsion of the arch-criminal, Catilina.*

7. O fortunatam rem publicam, si quidem hanc sentinam
urbis eiecerit ! Uno mehercule Catilina exhausto levata 10
mihi et recreata res publica videtur. Quid enim mali aut
sceleris fingi aut cogitari potest, quod non ille conceperit ?
quis tota Italia veneficus, quis gladiator, quis latro, quis
sicarius, quis parricida, quis testamentorum subiector, quis
circumscriptor, quis ganeo, quis nepos, quis adulter, quae 15
mulier infamis, quis corruptor iuventutis, quis corruptus,
quis perditus inveniri potest, qui se cum Catilina non
familiarissime vixisse fateatur ? Quae caedes per hosce
annos sine illo facta est ? quod nefarium stuprum non per
illum ?   20

*We are well rid of his wickedness and his fatal influence over all
desperate men.*

8. Iam vero quae tanta umquam in ullo iuventutis
illecebra fuit, quanta in illo ? qui alios ipse amabat turpis-
sime, aliorum amori flagitiosissime serviebat, aliis fructum
libidinum, aliis mortem parentum non modo impellendo,
verum etiam adiuvando pollicebatur. Nunc vero quam 25
subito non solum ex urbe, verum etiam ex agris ingentem
numerum perditorum hominum collegerat ! Nemo non
modo Romae, sed ne ullo quidem in angulo totius Italiae
oppressus aere alieno fuit, quem non ad hoc incredibile
sceleris foedus adsciverit.   30

V.

*He was the intimate friend of all the most worthless gladiators and
stage players. Would that they had followed him.*

9. Atque ut eius diversa studia in dissimili ratione perspicere possitis, nemo est in ludo gladiatorio paulo ad

facinus audacior, qui se non intimum Catilinae [esse
fateatur], nemo in scaena levior et nequior, qui se non
eiusdem prope sodalem fuisse commemoret. Atque idem 5
tamen, stuprorum et scelerum exercitatione adsuefactus
frigore et fame et siti et vigiliis perferendis, fortis ab istis
praedicabatur, cum industriae subsidia atque instrumenta
virtutis in libidine audaciaque consumeret. 10. Hunc
vero si secuti erunt sui comites, si ex urbe exierint des- 10
peratorum hominum flagitiosi greges, o nos beatos, o rem
publicam fortunatam, o praeclaram laudem consulatus mei !

They have abandoned themselves to violence, gluttony, and debauchery.

Non enim iam sunt mediocres hominum libidines, non
humanae et tolerandae audaciae: nihil cogitant nisi
caedem, nisi incendia, nisi rapinas. Patrimonia sua pro- 15
fuderunt, fortunas suas obligaverunt, res eos iam pridem,
fides nuper deficere coepit: eadem tamen illa, quae erat in
abundantia, libido permanet. Quodsi in vino et alea
comissationes solum et scorta quaererent, essent illi quidem
desperandi, sed tamen essent ferendi: hoc vero quis ferre 20
possit, inertes homines fortissimis viris insidiari, stultis-
simos prudentissimis, ebrios sobriis, dormientes vigilantibus? qui mihi accubantes in conviviis, complexi mulieres
impudicas, vino languidi, conferti cibo, sertis redimiti,
unguentis obliti, debilitati stupris, eructant sermonibus suis 25
caedem bonorum atque urbis incendia.

*But their punishment is at hand; I well know the danger, and I am
ready to meet it.*

11. Quibus ego confido impendere fatum aliquod et
poenam iam diu improbitati, nequitiae, sceleri, libidini
debitam aut instare iam plane aut certe appropinquare.
Quos si meus consulatus, quoniam sanare non potest, 30
sustulerit, non breve nescio quod tempus, sed multa saecula
propagarit rei publicae. Nulla est enim natio, quam
pertimescamus, nullus rex, qui bellum populo Romano
facere possit; omnia sunt externa unius virtute terra
marique pacata: domesticum bellum manet, intus insidiae 35

sunt, intus inclusum periculum est, intus est hostis: cum
luxuria nobis, cum amentia, cum scelere certandum est.
Huic ego me bello ducem profiteor, Quirites; suscipio
inimicitias hominum perditorum: quae sanari poterunt,
quacumque ratione sanabo; quae resecanda erunt, non 40
patiar ad perniciem civitatis manere. Proinde aut exeant
aut quiescant aut, si et in urbe et in eadem mente permanent, ea quae merentur exspectent.

VI.

*Others reproach me with having driven Catilina into exile. What I
did was to declare to the Senate—who showed their approval of what I
said—the details of his plans.*

12. At etiam sunt qui dicant, Quirites, a me eiectum in
exsilium esse Catilinam. Quod ego si verbo adsequi possem,
istos ipsos eicerem, qui haec loquuntur. Homo enim
videlicet timidus aut etiam permodestus vocem consulis
ferre non potuit; simul atque ire in exsilium iussus est, 5
paruit, ivit. Hesterno die, Quirites, cum domi meae paene
interfectus essem, senatum in aedem Iovis Statoris con-
vocavi, rem omnem ad patres conscriptos detuli: quo cum
Catilina venisset, quis eum senator appellavit? quis
salutavit? quis denique ita adspexit ut perditum civem, 10
ac non potius ut importunissimum hostem? quin etiam
principes eius ordinis partem illam subselliorum, ad quam
ille accesserat, nudam atque inanem reliquerunt.

*He made no attempt to deny my accusations, and I bade him betake
himself to the camp of Manlius, whither I knew he already meant to go.
Was that driving him into exile?*

13. Hic ego vehemens ille consul, qui verbo cives in
exsilium eicio, quaesivi a Catilina, in nocturno conventu 15
apud M. Laecam fuisset necne. Cum ille, homo audacis-
simus, conscientia convictus primo reticuisset, patefeci
cetera: quid ea nocte egisset, [ubi fuisset,] quid in proximam
constituisset, quem ad modum esset ei ratio totius belli

descripta, edocui.   Cum haesitaret, cum teneretur, quaesivi, 20
quid dubitaret proficisci eo, quo iam pridem pararet, cum
arma, cum secures, cum fasces, cum tubas, cum signa
militaria, cum aquilam illam argenteam, cui ille etiam
sacrarium domi suae fecerat, scirem esse praemissam.   14.
In exsilium eiciebam, quem iam ingressum esse in bellum 25
videbam ?   Etenim, credo, Manlius iste centurio, qui in
agro Faesulano castra posuit, bellum populo Romano suo
nomine indixit, et illa castra nunc non Catilinam ducem
exspectant, et ille eiectus in exsilium se Massiliam, ut
aiunt, non in haec castra conferet.   30

VII.

*Yet now if he should change his mind and really go into exile, I am
to be called a tyrant.*

O condicionem miseram non modo administrandae,
verum etiam conservandae rei publicae !   Nunc si L.
Catilina consiliis, laboribus, periculis meis circumclusus ac
debilitatus subito pertimuerit, sententiam mutaverit,
deseruerit suos, consilium belli faciendi abiecerit et ex hoc 5
cursu sceleris ac belli iter ad fugam atque in exsilium converterit, non ille a me spoliatus armis audaciae, non
obstupefactus ac perterritus mea diligentia, non de spe
conatuque depulsus, sed indemnatus, innocens in exsilium
eiectus a consule vi et minis esse dicetur, et erunt qui 10
illum, si hoc fecerit, non improbum, sed miserum, me
non diligentissimum consulem, sed crudelissimum tyran-
num existimari velint.

*I would gladly endure this if war might thus be averted.   But there is
no chance of it; in three days he will be in arms.*

15. Est mihi tanti, Quirites, huius invidiae falsae atque
iniquae tempestatem subire, dum modo a vobis huius 15
horribilis belli ac nefarii periculum depellatur.   Dicatur
sane eiectus esse a me, dum modo eat in exsilium: sed,

mihi credite, non est iturus. Numquam ego ab dis immortalibus optabo, Quirites, invidiae meae relevandae causa,
ut L. Catilinam ducere exercitum hostium atque in armis 20
volitare audiatis, sed triduo tamen audietis; multoque
magis illud timeo, ne mihi sit invidiosum aliquando, quod
illum emiserim potius quam quod eiecerim. Sed cum sint
homines, qui illum, cum profectus sit, eiectum esse dicant,
idem, si interfectus esset, quid dicerent ? 25

Those who reproach me are really his secret partisans.

16. Quamquam isti, qui Catilinam Massiliam ire dictitant,
non tam hoc queruntur quam verentur. Nemo est istorum
tam misericors, qui illum non ad Manlium quam ad Massi-
lienses ire malit. Ille autem, si mehercule hoc, quod agit,
numquam antea cogitasset, tamen latrocinantem se interfici 30
mallet quam exsulem vivere. Nunc vero, cum ei nihil
adhuc praeter ipsius voluntatem cogitationemque acciderit,
nisi quod vivis nobis Roma profectus est, optemus potius
ut eat in exsilium quam queramur.

VIII.

*But to turn from Catilina himself to his followers in Rome, I hope to
win some of them back to their loyalty.*

17. Sed cur tam diu de uno hoste loquimur, et de eo
hoste, qui iam fatetur se esse hostem et quem, quia, quod
semper volui, murus interest, non timeo: de his, qui
dissimulant, qui Romae remanent, qui nobiscum sunt,
nihil dicimus ? Quos quidem ego, si ullo modo fieri 5
possit, non tam ulcisci studeo quam sanare sibi ipsos,
placare rei publicae, neque id quare fieri non possit, si me
audire volent, intellego. Exponam enim vobis, Quirites,
ex quibus generibus hominum istae copiae comparentur;
deinde singulis medicinam consilii atque orationis meae, si 10
quam potero, adferam.

They may be divided into six classes, the first of which is composed of men with large debts, but larger estates, which they will not part with, hoping that Catilina will declare an abolition of debts. But their only chance is a compulsory sale, which I offer them.

18. Unum genus est eorum, qui magno in aere alieno maiores etiam possessiones habent, quarum amore adducti dissolvi nullo modo possunt. Horum hominum species est honestissima—sunt enim locupletes—, voluntas vero et 15 causa impudentissima. Tu agris, tu aedificiis, tu argento, tu familia, tu rebus omnibus ornatus et copiosus sis, et dubites de possessione detrahere, adquirere ad fidem ? Quid enim exspectas ? bellum ? Quid ergo ? in vastatione omnium tuas possessiones sacrosanctas futuras putas ? An 20 tabulas novas ? Errant qui istas a Catilina exspectant: meo beneficio tabulae novae proferentur, verum auctionariae; neque enim isti, qui possessiones habent, alia ratione ulla salvi esse possunt. Quod si maturius facere voluissent neque, id quod stultissimum est, certare cum usuris fructi- 25 bus praediorum, et locupletioribus his et melioribus civibus uteremur. Sed hosce homines minime puto pertimescendos, quod aut deduci de sententia possunt aut, si permanebunt, magis mihi videntur vota facturi contra rem publicam quam arma laturi.   30

IX.

Secondly, there are those who hope by a revolution to obtain power and office. Let these men mark well the forces opposed to them, and remember that even if the revolution succeeded, the chief power would not fall to them.

19. Alterum genus est eorum, qui, quamquam premuntur aere alieno, dominationem tamen exspectant, rerum potiri volunt, honores, quos quieta re publica desperant, perturbata se consequi posse arbitrantur. Quibus hoc praecipiendum videtur, unum scilicet et idem quod reliquis 5 omnibus, ut desperent se id quod conantur consequi posse: primum omnium me ipsum vigilare, adesse, providere rei publicae; deinde magnos animos esse in bonis viris,

magnam concordiam in maxima multitudine, magnas
praeterea militum copias; deos denique immortales huic 10
invicto populo, clarissimo imperio, pulcherrimae urbi
contra tantam vim sceleris praesentes auxilium esse
laturos. Quodsi iam sint id, quod summo furore cupiunt,
adepti, num illi in cinere urbis et in sanguine civium, quae
mente conscelerata ac nefaria concupiverunt, consules se aut 15
dictatores aut etiam reges sperant futuros ? Non vident id
se cupere, quod si adepti sint, fugitivo alicui aut gladiatori
concedi sit necesse ?

*Thirdly, the Sullan colonists, who want fresh chances of plunder.
But the State will not endure the horrors of another proscription.*

20. Tertium genus est aetate iam adfectum, sed tamen
exercitatione robustum, quo ex genere iste est Manlius, cui 20
nunc Catilina succedit. Hi sunt homines ex iis coloniis,
quas Sulla constituit: quas ego universas civium esse
optimorum st fortissimorum virorum sentio, sed tamen
ii sunt coloni, qui se in insperatis ac repentinis pecuniis
sumptuosius insolentiusque iactarunt. Hi dum aedificant 25
tamquam beati, dum praediis, lecticis, familiis magnis, conviviis apparatis delectantur, in tantum aes alienum incider-
unt, ut, si salvi esse velint, Sulla sit iis ab inferis excitandus:
qui etiam nonnullos agrestes, homines tenues atque egentes
in eandem illam spem rapinarum veterum impulerunt. Quos 30
ego utrosque in eodem genere praedatorum direptorumque
pono, sed eos hoc moneo: desinant furere ac proscriptiones
et dictaturas cogitare. Tantus enim illorum temporum dolor
inustus est civitati, ut iam ista non modo homines, sed ne
pecudes quidem mihi passurae esse videantur. 35

X.

*Fourthly, the hopeless bankrupts. Their ruin is certain, but they
need not involve the whole State in it.*

21. Quartum genus est sane varium et mixtum et turbulentum, qui iam pridem premuntur, qui numquam emer-

42   CICERO

gunt, qui partim inertia, partim male gerendo negotio,
partim etiam sumptibus in vetere aere alieno vacillant, qui
vadimoniis, iudiciis, proscriptione bonorum defatigati, 5
permulti et ex urbe et ex agris se in illa castra conferre
dicuntur. Hosce ego non tam milites acres quam infitiatores lentos esse arbitror. Qui homines quam primum,
si stare non possunt, corruant, sed ita, ut non modo civitas,
sed ne vicini quidem proximi sentiant. Nam illud non 10
intellego, quam ob rem, si vivere honeste non possunt,
perire turpiter velint, aut cur minore dolore perituros se
cum multis, quam si soli pereant, arbitrentur.

*Fifthly, the criminals of every class; let them stay with Catilina and
perish with him.*

22. Quintum genus est parricidarum, sicariorum, denique
omnium facinorosorum: quos ego a Catilina non revoco; 15
nam neque ab eo divelli possunt et pereant sane in latrocinio,
quoniam sunt ita multi, ut eos carcer capere non possit.

*Lastly, there are the dissolute youths of Rome. If they are not
destroyed or banished, another Catilina will arise among them.*

Postremum autem genus est, non solum numero, verum
etiam genere ipso atque vita, quod proprium Catilinae est,
de eius dilectu, immo vero de complexu eius ac sinu, quos 20
pexo capillo nitidos aut imberbes aut bene barbatos videtis,
manicatis et talaribus tunicis, velis amictos, non togis,
quorum omnis industria vitae et vigilandi labor in antelu-
canis cenis expromitur. 23. In his gregibus omnes
aleatores, omnes adulteri, omnes impuri impudicique 25
versantur. Hi pueri tam lepidi ac delicati non solum amare
et amari, neque cantare et saltare, sed etiam sicas vibrare
et spargere venena didicerunt: qui nisi exeunt, nisi pereunt,
etiam si Catilina perierit, scitote hoc in re publica seminarium Catilinarum futurum. Verum tamen quid sibi isti 30
miseri volunt ? num suas secum mulierculas sunt in castra
ducturi ? Quem ad modum autem illis carere poterunt,
his praesertim iam noctibus ? quo autem pacto illi Appenninum atque illas pruinas ac nives perferent ? nisi idcirco

se facilius hiemem toleraturos putant, quod nudi in con- 35
viviis saltare didicerunt.

XI.

*We scarcely need the armies of the State to defeat such contemptible
opponents.*

24. O bellum magno opere pertimescendum, cum hanc
sit habiturus Catilina scortorum cohortem praetoriam !
Instruite nunc, Quirites, contra has tam praeclaras Catilinae
copias vestra praesidia vestrosque exercitus: et primum
gladiatori illi confecto et saucio consules imperatoresque 5
vestros opponite; deinde contra illam naufragorum eiectam
ac debilitatam manum florem totius Italiae ac robur educite.
Iam vero urbes coloniarum ac municipiorum respondebunt
Catilinae tumulis silvestribus. Neque ego ceteras copias,
ornamenta, praesidia vestra cum illius latronis inopia atque 10
egestate conferre debeo.

*We have all the resources of the government, while they have nothing.
Moreover, ours is the cause of good against evil, and in such a contest
the result is certain.*

25. Sed si omissis his rebus, quibus nos suppeditamur,
eget ille, senatu, equitibus Romanis, urbe, aerario, vectigalibus, cuncta Italia, provinciis omnibus, exteris nationibus,
si his rebus omissis causas ipsas, quae inter se confligunt, 15
contendere velimus, ex eo ipso, quam valde illi iaceant,
intellegere possumus. Ex hac enim parte pudor pugnat,
illinc petulantia; hinc pudicitia, illinc stuprum; hinc fides,
illinc fraudatio; hinc pietas, illinc scelus; hinc constantia,
illinc furor; hinc honestas, illinc turpitudo; hinc continen- 20
tia, illinc libido; denique aequitas, temperantia, fortitudo,
prudentia, virtutes omnes certant cum iniquitate, luxuria,
ignavia, temeritate, cum vitiis omnibus; postremo copia
cum egestate, bona ratio cum perdita, mens sana cum
amentia, bona denique spes cum omnium rerum despera- 25
tione confligit. In eius modi certamine ac proelio nonne, si

hominum studia deficiant, di ipsi immortales cogant ab his praeclarissimis virtutibus tot et tanta vitia superari?

XII.

I advise you, then, to guard your own homes. The protection of the city shall be my care. Q. Metellus will at least hold the rebels in check.

26. Quae cum ita sint, Quirites, vos, quem ad modum iam antea dixi, vestra tecta vigiliis custodiisque defendite: mihi, ut urbi sine vestro motu ac sine ullo tumultu satis esset praesidii, consultum atque provisum est. Coloni omnes municipesque vestri, certiores a me facti de hac 5 nocturna excursione Catilinae, facile urbes suas finesque defendent. Gladiatores, quam sibi ille manum certissimam fore putavit—quamquam animo meliore sunt quam pars patriciorum—, potestate tamen nostra continebuntur. Q. Metellus, quem ego hoc prospiciens in agrum Gallicum 10 Picenumque praemisi, aut opprimet hominem aut eius omnes motus conatusque prohibebit. Reliquis autem de rebus constituendis, maturandis, agendis iam ad senatum referemus, quem vocari videtis.

One final warning to Catilina's partisans within the city. I am willing to allow them to leave Rome, but if they remain, the slightest attempt at conspiracy will be detected and punished.

27. Nunc illos, qui in urbe remanserunt, atque adeo qui 15 contra urbis salutem omniumque vestrum in urbe a Catilina relicti sunt, quamquam sunt hostes, tamen, quia sunt cives, monitos etiam atque etiam volo. Mea lenitas adhuc si cui solutior visa est, hoc exspectavit, ut id, quod latebat, erumperet. Quod reliquum est, iam non possum 20 oblivisci, meam hanc esse patriam, me horum esse consulem, mihi aut cum his vivendum aut pro his esse moriendum. Nullus est portis custos, nullus insidiator viae; si qui exire volunt, conivere possum: qui vero se in urbe commoverit, cuius ego non modo factum, sed incep- 25 tum ullum conatumve contra patriam deprehendero,

sentiet in hac urbe esse consules vigilantes, esse egregios
magistratus, esse fortem senatum, esse arma, esse carcerem,
quem vindicem nefariorum ac manifestorum scelerum
maiores nostri esse voluerunt.   30

XIII.

*All this shall be done with the least possible disturbance and severity.
I place my trust in the gods and I bid you also address your prayers to
them.*

28. Atque haec omnia sic agentur, Quirites, ut maximae
res minimo motu, pericula summa nullo tumultu, bellum
intestinum ac domesticum post hominum memoriam crudelissimum et maximum me uno togato duce et imperatore
sedetur.   Quod ego sic administrabo, Quirites, ut, si ullo 5
modo fieri poterit, ne improbus quidem quisquam in hac
urbe poenam sui sceleris sufferat.   Sed si vis manifestae
audaciae, si impendens patriae periculum me necessario de
hac animi lenitate deduxerit, illud profecto perficiam, quod
in tanto et tam insidioso bello vix optandum videtur, ut 10
neque bonus quisquam intereat paucorumque poena vos
omnes salvi esse possitis.   29. Quae quidem ego neque mea
prudentia neque humanis consiliis fretus polliceor vobis,
Quirites, sed multis et non dubiis deorum immortalium
significationibus, quibus ego ducibus in hanc spem senten- 15
tiamque sum ingressus: qui iam non procul, ut quondam
solebant, ab externo hoste atque longinquo, sed hic praesentes suo numine atque auxilio sua templa atque urbis
tecta defendunt.   Quos vos, Quirites, precari, venerari,
implorare debetis, ut, quam urbem pulcherrimam floren- 20
tissimamque esse voluerunt, hanc omnibus hostium copiis
terra marique superatis a perditissimorum civium nefario
scelere defendant.

M. TULLI CICERONIS
IN CATILINAM ORATIO TERTIA
HABITA AD POPULUM.

I.

Citizens of Rome, I have saved the State, and may claim equal honour with its founder.

Rem publicam, Quirites, vitamque omnium vestrum, bona fortunas, coniuges liberosque vestros atque hoc domicilium clarissimi imperii, fortunatissimam pulcherrimamque urbem hodierno die deorum immortalium summo erga vos amore, laboribus, consiliis, periculis meis e flamma atque 5 ferro ac paene ex faucibus fati ereptam et vobis conservatam ac restitutam videtis. 2. Et si non minus nobis iucundi atque illustres sunt ii dies, quibus conservamur, quam illi, quibus nascimur, quod salutis certa laetitia est, nascendi incerta condicio, et quod sine sensu nascimur, cum voluptate 10 servamur, profecto, quoniam illum, qui hanc urbem condidit, ad deos immortales benevolentia famaque sustulimus, esse apud vos posterosque vestros in honore debebit is, qui eandem hanc urbem conditam amplificatamque servavit. Nam toti urbi, templis delubris, tectis ac moenibus subiectos 15 prope iam ignes circumdatosque restinximus, idemque gladios in rem publicam destrictos rettudimus mucronesque eorum a iugulis vestris deiecimus.

Ever since Catilina took to flight I have been constantly on the watch for evidence against his confederates.

3. Quae quoniam in senatu illustrata, patefacta, comperta sunt per me, vobis iam exponam breviter, Quirites, ut et 20 quanta et quam manifesta et qua ratione investigata et

46

comprehensa sint, vos, qui et ignoratis et exspectatis, scire
possitis. Principio, ut Catilina paucis ante diebus erupit
ex urbe, cum sceleris sui socios, huiusce nefarii belli acer-
rimos duces, Romae reliquisset, semper vigilavi et providi, 25
Quirites, quem ad modum in tantis et tam absconditis
insidiis salvi esse possemus.

II.

*For I found that the other conspirators did not leave Rome with
Catilina. Accordingly I waited for proof to convict them and convince
you of your danger.*

Nam tum, cum ex urbe Catilinam eiciebam—non enim
iam vereor huius verbi invidiam, cum illa magis sit timenda,
quod vivus exierit,—sed tum, cum illum exterminari
volebam, aut reliquam coniuratorum manum simul exituram
aut eos, qui restitissent, infirmos sine illo ac debiles fore 5
putabam. 4. Atque ego ut vidi, quos maximo furore et
scelere esse inflammatos sciebam, eos nobiscum esse et
Romae remansisse, in eo omnes dies noctesque consumpsi,
ut, quid agerent, quid molirentur, sentirem ac viderem, ut,
quoniam auribus vestris propter incredibilem magnitudinem 10
sceleris minorem fidem faceret oratio mea, rem ita comprehenderem, ut tum demum animis saluti vestrae provide-
retis, cum oculis maleficium ipsum videretis.

*This came at last when Lentulus and others fatally compromised them-
selves by entrusting their secrets to the envoys of the Allobroges.*

Itaque ut comperi, legatos Allobrogum belli Transalpini
et tumultus Gallici excitandi causa a P. Lentulo esse sollici- 15
tatos, eosque in Galliam ad suos cives eodemque itinere cum
litteris mandatisque ad Catilinam esse missos, comitemque
iis adiunctum esse T. Volturcium atque huic esse ad Catilinam
datas litteras, facultatem mihi oblatam putavi, ut, quod
erat difficillimum quodque ego semper optabam ab dis 20

immortalibus, tota res non solum a me, sed etiam a senatu
et a vobis manifesto deprehenderetur.

*I sent an armed force to the Mulvian bridge to intercept these envoys,
with whom was Volturcius, the agent of Lentulus.*

5. Itaque hesterno die L. Flaccum et C. Pomptinum
praetores, fortissimos atque amantissimos rei publicae viros,
ad me vocavi, rem exposui, quid fieri placeret ostendi. Illi 25
autem, qui omnia de re publica praeclara atque egregia
sentirent, sine recusatione ac sine ulla mora negotium
susceperunt et, cum advesperasceret, occulte ad pontem
Mulvium pervenerunt atque ibi in proximis villis ita
bipertito fuerunt, ut Tiberis inter eos et pons interesset. 30
Eodem autem et ipsi sine cuiusquam suspicione multos
fortes viros eduxerant, et ego ex praefectura Reatina complures delectos adulescentes, quorum opera utor adsidue in
rei publicae praesidio, cum gladiis miseram. 6. Interim
tertia fere vigilia exacta, cum iam pontem Mulvium magno 35
comitatu legati Allobrogum ingredi inciperent unaque
Volturcius, fit in eos impetus; educuntur et ab illis gladii
et a nostris. Res praetoribus erat nota solis, ignorabatur
a ceteris.

III.

*They were all arrested, and the letters brought to me unopened. I
then summoned to my presence Lentulus, Cethegus, Statilius, and
Gabinius.*

Tum interventu Pomptini atque Flacci pugna, quae erat
commissa, sedatur. Litterae, quaecumque erant in eo comitatu, integris signis praetoribus traduntur; ipsi compre-
hensi ad me, cum iam dilucesceret, deducuntur. Atque
horum omnium scelerum improbissimum machinatorem 5
Cimbrum Gabinium statim ad me, nihildum suspicantem,
vocavi; deinde item accersitus est L. Statilius et post eum
C. Cethegus; tardissime autem Lentulus venit, credo, quod
in litteris dandis praeter consuetudinem proxima nocte
vigilarat.   10

*Then, wishing to deal openly with the whole matter, I convoked the
Senate. Meanwhile I had the house of Cethegus searched for weapons,
of which a large quantity were found.*

7. Cum summis et clarissimis huius civitatis viris, qui
audita re frequentes ad me mane convenerant, litteras a
me prius aperiri quam ad senatum deferri placeret ne, si
nihil esset inventum, temere a me tantus tumultus iniectus
civitati videretur, negavi me esse facturum, ut de periculo 15
publico non ad consilium publicum rem integram deferrem.
Etenim, Quirites, si ea, quae erant ad me delata, reperta
non essent, tamen ego non arbitrabar in tantis rei publicae
periculis esse mihi nimiam diligentiam pertimescendam.
Senatum frequentem celeriter, ut vidistis, coëgi. 8. Atque 20
interea statim admonitu Allobrogum C. Sulpicium praetorem, fortem virum, misi, qui ex aedibus Cethegi, si quid
telorum esset, efferret, ex quibus ille maximum sicarum
numerum et gladiorum extulit.

IV.

*Before the Senate Volturcius confessed that he had received from
Lentulus a letter for Catilina, bidding him come to Rome with all speed,
in order to cut off the fugitives when the massacre began.*

Introduxi Volturcium sine Gallis, fidem publicam iussu
senatus dedi, hortatus sum ut ea quae sciret sine timore
indicaret. Tum ille dixit, cum vix se ex magno timore
recreasset, a P. Lentulo se habere ad Catilinam mandata
et litteras, ut servorum praesidio uteretur, ut ad urbem 5
quam primum cum exercitu accederet; id autem eo consilio,
ut, cum urbem ex omnibus partibus, quem ad modum
discriptum distributumque erat, incendissent caedemque
infinitam civium fecissent, praesto esset ille, qui et fugientes
exciperet et se cum his urbanis ducibus coniungeret. 10

*The Gauls then disclosed the fact that they had been ordered to furnish
cavalry for the conspirators, and that Lentulus had told them that the
prophetic books had foretold his supremacy at Rome.*

9. Introducti autem Galli ius iurandum sibi et litteras ab
Lentulo, Cethego, Statilio ad suam gentem data esse dixe-

runt, atque ita sibi ab his et a L. Cassio esse praescriptum,
ut equitatum in Italiam quam primum mitterent; pedestres
sibi copias non defuturas; Lentulum autem sibi confir- 15
masse ex fatis Sibyllinis haruspicumque responsis, se esse
tertium illum Cornelium, ad quem regnum huius urbis
atque imperium pervenire esset necesse; Cinnam ante se
et Sullam fuisse: eundemque dixisse fatalem hunc annum
esse ad interitum huius urbis atque imperii, qui esset annus 20
decimus post virginum absolutionem, post Capitolii autem
incensionem vicesimum. 10. Hanc autem Cethego cum
ceteris controversiam fuisse dixerunt, quod Lentulo et aliis
Saturnalibus caedem fieri atque urbem incendi placeret,
Cethego nimium id longum videretur. 25

V.

The letters, which their writers, Lentulus, Statilius, and Cethegus,
were forced to acknowledge, were found to confirm the evidence already
received.

Ac ne longum sit, Quirites, tabellas proferri iussimus,
quae a quoque dicebantur datae. Primo ostendimus
Cethego signum; cognovit; nos linum incidimus, legimus.
Erat scriptum ipsius manu Allobrogum senatui et populo,
sese quae eorum legatis confirmasset facturum esse; orare 5
ut item illi facerent quae sibi eorum legati recepissent.
Tum Cethegus, qui paulo ante aliquid tamen de gladiis ac
sicis, quae apud ipsum erant deprehensa, respondisset
dixissetque se semper bonorum ferramentorum studiosum
fuisse, recitatis litteris debilitatus atque abiectus conscientia 10
repente conticuit. Introductus est Statilius; cognovit et
signum et manum suam; recitatae sunt tabellae in eandem
fere sententiam; confessus est. Tum ostendi tabellas Lentulo et quaesivi, cognosceretne signum. Adnuit. "Est
vero" inquam "notum quidem signum, imago avi tui, 15
clarissimi viri, qui amavit unice patriam et cives suos, quae
quidem te a tanto scelere etiam muta revocare debuit."

Lentulus tried to cross-examine the Gauls, but finally broke down.

11. Leguntur eadem ratione ad senatum Allobrogum populumque litterae. Si quid de his rebus dicere vellet, feci potestatem. Atque ille primo quidem negavit; post 20 autem aliquanto, toto iam indicio exposito atque edito, surrexit, quaesivit a Gallis, quid sibi esset cum iis, quam ob rem domum suam venissent, itemque a Volturcio. Qui cum illi breviter constanterque respondissent, per quem ad eum quotiensque venissent, quaesissentque ab eo, nihilne 25 secum esset de fatis Sibyllinis locutus, tum ille subito scelere demens, quanta conscientiae vis esset, ostendit: nam cum id posset infitiari, repente praeter opinionem omnium confessus est. Ita eum non modo ingenium illud et dicendi exercitatio, qua semper valuit, sed etiam propter vim 30 sceleris manifesti atque deprehensi impudentia, qua superabat omnes, improbitasque defecit.

His letter to Catilina was then produced and acknowledged by him. Lastly Gabinius also confessed his guilt. In addition to these outward proofs the cowed demeanour of the conspirators now revealed their treason.

12. Volturcius vero subito litteras proferri atque aperiri iubet, quas sibi a Lentulo ad Catilinam datas esse dicebat. Atque ibi vehementissime perturbatus Lentulus tamen et 35 signum et manum suam cognovit. Erant autem sine nomine, sed ita: " Quis sim, scies ex eo, quem ad te misi. Cura ut vir sis et cogita, quem in locum sis progressus; vide, quid tibi iam sit necesse, et cura ut omnium tibi auxilia adiungas, etiam infimorum." Gabinius deinde 40 introductus, cum primo impudenter respondere coepisset, ad extremum nihil ex iis, quae Galli insimulabant, negavit. 13. Ac mihi quidem, Quirites, cum illa certissima visa sunt argumenta atque indicia sceleris, tabellae, signa, manus, denique unius cuiusque confessio, tum multo certiora illa, 45 color, oculi, vultus, taciturnitas. Sic enim obstupuerant, sic terram intuebantur, sic furtim nonnumquam inter sese adspiciebant, ut non iam ab aliis indicari, sed indicare se ipsi viderentur.

VI.

The Senate then passed a vote of thanks to me, to my colleague, and to the praetors.

Indiciis expositis atque editis, Quirites, senatum con-
sului, de summa re publica quid fieri placeret. Dictae sunt
a principibus acerrimae ac fortissimae sententiae, quas
senatus sine ulla varietate est secutus. Et quoniam nondum est perscriptum senatus consultum, ex memoria vobis, 5
Quirites, quid senatus censuerit exponam. 14. Primum
mihi gratiae verbis amplissimis aguntur, quod virtute,
consilio, providentia mea res publica maximis periculis sit
liberata; deinde L. Flaccus et C. Pomptinus praetores,
quod eorum opera forti fidelique usus essem, merito ac iure 10
laudantur; atque etiam viro forti, collegae meo, laus im-
pertitur, quod eos, qui huius coniurationis participes fuis-
sent, a suis et a rei publicae consiliis removisset.

Lentulus and eight others were then placed under arrest.

Atque ita censuerunt, ut P. Lentulus, cum se praetura
abdicasset, in custodiam traderetur; itemque uti C. 15
Cethegus, L. Statilius, P. Gabinius, qui omnes praesentes
erant, in custodiam traderentur; atque idem hoc decretum
est in L. Cassium, qui sibi procurationem incendendae
urbis depoposcerat, in M. Ceparium, cui ad sollicitandos
pastores Apuliam attributam esse erat indicatum, in P. 20
Furium, qui est ex iis colonis, quos Faesulas L. Sulla
deduxit, in Q. Annium Chilonem, qui una cum hoc Furio
semper erat in hac Allobrogum sollicitatione versatus, in P.
Umbrenum, libertinum hominem, a quo primum Gallos ad
Gabinium perductos esse constabat. 25

*The Senate then decreed a public thanksgiving in my honour, an
unprecedented distinction for a civilian.*

15. Atque ea lenitate senatus est usus, Quirites, ut ex
tanta coniuratione tantaque hac multitudine domesticorum
hostium novem hominum perditissimorum poena re publica
conservata, reliquorum mentes sanari posse arbitraretur.
Atque etiam supplicatio dis immortalibus pro singulari 30

eorum merito meo nomine decreta est, quod mihi primum
post hanc urbem conditam togato contigit, et his decreta
verbis est " quod urbem incendiis, caede cives, Italiam
bello liberassem." Quae supplicatio si cum ceteris suppli-
cationibus conferatur, hoc interest, quod ceterae bene gesta, 35
haec una conservata re publica constituta est. Atque
illud, quod faciendum primum fuit, factum atque trans-
actum est. Nam P. Lentulus, quamquam patefactis
indiciis, confessionibus suis, iudicio senatus non modo
praetoris ius, verum etiam civis amiserat, tamen magistratu 40
se abdicavit, ut, quae religio C. Mario, clarissimo viro, non
fuerat quo minus C. Glauciam, de quo nihil nominatim erat
decretum, praetorem occideret, ea nos religione in privato
P. Lentulo puniendo liberaremur.

VII.

*By the capture of his confederates in the city Catilina's cause is
ruined. Now that he is not here to lead them I do not fear those that
remain.*

16. Nunc quoniam, Quirites, consceleratissimi pericu-
losissimique belli nefarios duces captos iam et comprehensos
tenetis, existimare debetis, omnes Catilinae copias, omnes
spes atque opes his depulsis urbis periculis concidisse.
Quem quidem ego cum ex urbe pellebam, hoc providebam 5
animo, Quirites, remoto Catilina non mihi esse P. Lentuli
somnum nec L. Cassii adipes nec C. Cethegi furiosam
temeritatem pertimescendam. Ille erat unus timendus ex
istis omnibus, sed tam diu, dum urbis moenibus contine-
batur. Omnia norat, omnium aditus tenebat; appellare, 10
temptare, sollicitare poterat, audebat; erat ei consilium ad
facinus aptum, consilio autem neque lingua neque manus
deerat. Iam ad certas res conficiendas certos homines
delectos ac descriptos habebat. Neque vero, cum aliquid
mandarat, confectum putebat: nihil erat quod non ipse 15
obiret occurreret, vigilaret laboraret; frigus, sitim, famem
ferre poterat.

If Catilina had remained in Rome, the struggle would have been much more severe; we should have been forced to fight to the bitter end.

17. Hunc ego hominem tam acrem, tam audacem, tam paratum, tam callidum, tam in scelere vigilantem, tam in perditis rebus diligentem nisi ex domesticis insidiis in 20 castrense latrocinium compulissem—dicam id quod sentio, Quirites—non facile hanc tantam molem mali a cervicibus vestris depulissem. Non ille nobis Saturnalia constituisset neque tanto ante exitii ac fati diem rei publicae denuntia-visset, neque commisisset ut signum, ut litterae suae testes 25 manifesti sceleris deprehenderentur. Quae nunc illo absente sic gesta sunt, ut nullum in privata domo furtum umquam sit tam palam inventum, quam haec tanta in re publica coniuratio manifesto inventa atque deprehensa est. Quodsi Catilina in urbe ad hanc diem remansisset, quam-30 quam, quoad fuit, omnibus eius consiliis occurri atque obstiti, tamen, ut levissime dicam, dimicandum nobis cum illo fuisset, neque nos umquam, cum ille in urbe hostis esset, tantis periculis rem publicam tanta pace, tanto otio, tanto silentio liberassemus.   35

VIII.

Many signs show that the gods have had us under their special protection.

18. Quamquam haec omnia, Quirites, ita sunt a me admi-nistrata, ut deorum immortalium nutu atque consilio et gesta et provisa esse videantur; idque cum coniectura consequi possumus, quod vix videtur humani consilii tan-tarum rerum gubernatio esse potuisse, tum vero ita prae- 5 sentes his temporibus opem et auxilium nobis tulerunt, ut eos paene oculis videre possemus. Nam ut illa omittam, visas nocturno tempore ab occidente faces ardoremque caeli, ut fulminum iactus, ut terrae motus relinquam, ut omittam cetera, quae tam multa nobis consulibus facta sunt, 10 ut haec, quae nunc fiunt, canere di immortales viderentur, hoc certe, quod sum dicturus, neque praetermittendum neque relinquendum est.

The soothsayers warned us of our danger two years ago, when the Capitol was struck by lightning.

19. Nam profecto memoria tenetis, Cotta et Torquato consulibus complures in Capitolio res de caelo esse percussas, 15 cum et simulacra deorum depulsa sunt et statuae veterum hominum deiectae et legum aera liquefacta et tactus etiam ille, qui hanc urbem condidit, Romulus, quem inauratum in Capitolio, parvum atque lactantem, uberibus lupinis inhiantem, fuisse meministis. Quo quidem tempore cum 20 haruspices ex tota Etruria convenissent, caedes atque incendia et legum interitum et bellum civile ac domesticum et totius urbis atque imperii occasum appropinquare dixerunt, nisi di immortales omni ratione placati suo numine prope fata ipsa flexissent. 25

They bade us avert this danger by making a new statue of Jupiter, and turning it towards the Forum.

20. Itaque illorum responsis tum et ludi per decem dies facti sunt, neque res ulla, quae ad placandos deos pertineret, praetermissa est: idemque iusserunt simulacrum Iovis facere maius et in excelso collocare et, contra atque antea fuerat, ad orientem convertere; ac se sperare dixerunt, si 30 illud signum, quod videtis, solis ortum et forum curiamque conspiceret, fore ut ea consilia, quae clam essent inita contra salutem urbis atque imperii, illustrarentur, ut a senatu populoque Romano perspici possent. Atque illud signum collocandum consules illi locaverunt, sed tanta fuit 35 operis tarditas, ut neque superioribus consulibus neque nobis ante hodiernum diem collocaretur.

IX.

The gods are clearly on our side. At the very moment when the conspiracy was being detected the statue of Jupiter was being placed in position.

21. Hic quis potest esse, Quirites, tam aversus a vero, tam praeceps, tam mente captus, qui neget haec omnia,

quae videmus, praecipueque hanc urbem deorum immortalium nutu ac potestate administrari ? Etenim cum esset
ita responsum, caedes, incendia, interitum rei publicae com-   5
parari, et ea per cives: quae tum propter magnitudinem
scelerum nonnullis incredibilia videbantur, ea non modo
cogitata a nefariis civibus, verum etiam suscepta esse
sensistis. Illud vero nonne ita praesens est, ut nutu Iovis
Optimi Maximi factum esse videatur, ut, cum hodierno die 10
mane per forum meo iussu et coniurati et eorum indices
in aedem Concordiae ducerentur, eo ipso tempore signum
statueretur ? quo collocato atque ad vos senatumque con-
verso, omnia et senatus et vos, quae erant contra salutem
omnium cogitata, illustrata et patefacta vidistis.   15

*It is Jupiter who has saved Rome; it is he who gave me strength to
act, and he who caused the plotters to place their trust in the fickle Gauls.*

22. Quo etiam maiore sunt isti odio supplicioque digni,
qui non solum vestris domiciliis atque tectis, sed etiam
deorum templis atque delubris sunt funestos ac nefarios
ignes inferre conati. Quibus ego si me restitisse dicam,
nimium mihi sumam et non sim ferendus: ille, ille Iuppiter 20
restitit; ille Capitolium, ille haec templa, ille cunctam
urbem, ille vos omnes salvos esse voluit. Dis ego immortalibus ducibus hanc mentem, Quirites, voluntatemque
suscepi atque ad haec tanta indicia perveni. Iam vero ab
Lentulo ceterisque domesticis hostibus tam dementer tantae 25
res creditae et ignotis et barbaris commissaeque litterae
numquam essent profecto, nisi ab dis immortalibus huic
tantae audaciae consilium esset ereptum. Quid vero ? ut
homines Galli ex civitate male pacata, quae gens una restat,
quae bellum populo Romano facere posse et non nolle 30
videatur, spem imperii ac rerum maximarum ultro sibi a
patriciis hominibus oblatam neglegerent vestramque salutem suis opibus anteponerent, id non divinitus esse factum
putatis, praesertim qui nos non pugnando, sed tacendo
superare potuerint ?   35

X.

Celebrate, then, the thanksgiving: never was one better deserved.

23. Quam ob rem, Quirites, quoniam ad omnia pulvinaria supplicatio decreta est, celebratote illos dies cum coniugibus ac liberis vestris. Nam multi saepe honores dis immortalibus iusti habiti sunt ac debiti, sed profecto iustiores numquam. Erepti enim estis ex crudelissimo ac miserrimo interitu, erepti 5 sine caede, sine sanguine, sine exercitu, sine dimicatione; togati me uno togato duce et imperatore vicistis.

There have been many civil conflicts in the last twenty years, and much bloodshed.

24. Etenim recordamini, Quirites, omnes civiles dissensiones, non solum eas, quas audistis, sed eas, quas vosmet ipsi meministis atque vidistis. L. Sulla P. Sulpicium 10 oppressit: C. Marium, custodem huius urbis, multosque fortes viros partim eiecit ex civitate, partim interemit. Cn. Octavius consul armis expulit ex urbe collegam: omnis hic locus acervis corporum et civium sanguine redundavit. Superavit postea Cinna cum Mario: tum vero, clarissimis 15 viris interfectis, lumina civitatis exstincta sunt. Ultus est huius victoriae crudelitatem postea Sulla, ne dici quidem opus est, quanta deminutione civium et quanta calamitate rei publicae. Dissensit M. Lepidus a clarissimo et fortissimo viro Q. Catulo: attulit non tam ipsius interitus rei 20 publicae luctum quam ceterorum. •

But in these revolution was the object, not the destruction of the State.

25. Atque illae tamen omnes dissensiones erant eius modi, Quirites, quae non ad delendam, sed ad commutandam rem publicam pertinerent. Non illi nullam esse rem publicam, sed in ea, quae esset, se esse principes, neque 25 hanc urbem conflagrare, sed se in hac urbe florere voluerunt. Atque illae tamen omnes dissensiones, quarum nulla exitium rei publicae quaesivit, eius modi fuerunt, ut non reconciliatione concordiae, sed internecione civium diiudicatae sint. In hoc autem uno post hominum memoriam 30

maximo crudelissimoque bello, quale bellum nulla umquam
barbaria cum sua gente gessit, quo in bello lex haec fuit a
Lentulo, Catilina, Cethego, Cassio constituta, ut omnes, qui
salva urbe salvi esse possent, in hostium numero ducerentur,
ita me gessi, Quirites, ut salvi omnes conservaremini, et, 35
cum hostes vestri tantum civium superfuturum putassent,
quantum infinitae caedi restitisset, tantum autem urbis,
quantum flamma obire non potuisset, et urbem et cives
integros incolumesque servavi.

XI.

I ask no reward but your remembrance of what I have done for you.

26. Quibus pro tantis rebus, Quirites, nullum ego a vobis
praemium virtutis, nullum insigne honoris, nullum monumentum laudis postulabo praeterquam huius diei memoriam
sempiternam. In animis ego vestris omnes triumphos meos,
omnia ornamenta honoris, monumenta gloriae, laudis insig- 5
nia condi et collocari volo. Nihil me mutum potest delectare, nihil tacitum, nihil denique eius modi, quod etiam
minus digni adsequi possint. Memoria vestra, Quirites,
nostrae res alentur, sermonibus crescent, litterarum monumentis inveterascent et corroborabuntur; eandemque diem 10
intellego, quam spero aeternam fore, propagatam esse et ad
salutem urbis et ad memoriam consulatus mei, unoque
tempore in hac re publica duos cives exstitisse, quorum
alter fines vestri imperii non terrae, sed caeli regionibus
terminaret, alter eiusdem imperii domicilium sedesque 15
servaret.

XII.

*But since, unlike foreign conquerors, I must live side by side with my
enemies, see to it that I do not suffer from the hatred of those from whom
I have protected you.*

27. Sed quoniam earum rerum, quas ego gessi, non eadem
est fortuna atque condicio quae illorum, qui externa bella
gesserunt, quod mihi cum iis vivendum est, quos vici ac
subegi, illi hostes aut interfectos aut oppressos reliquerunt,

vestrum est, Quirites, si ceteris facta sua recte prosunt, 5
mihi mea ne quando obsint providere. Mentes enim
hominum audacissimorum sceleratae ac nefariae ne vobis
nocere possent ego providi: ne mihi noceant vestrum est
providere. Quamquam, Quirites, mihi quidem ipsi nihil
ab istis iam noceri potest. Magnum enim est in bonis 10
praesidium, quod mihi in perpetuum comparatum est,
magna in re publica dignitas, quae me semper tacita
defendet, magna vis conscientiae, quam qui neglegunt, cum
me violare volent, se indicabunt.

*Life can give me no greater honour than the glory I have won; I
will strive in future to be worthy of it.*

28. Est etiam in nobis is animus, Quirites, ut non modo 15
nullius audaciae cedamus, sed etiam omnes improbos ultro
semper lacessamus. Quodsi omnis impetus domesticorum
hostium, depulsus a vobis, se in me unum converterit, vobis
erit videndum, Quirites, qua condicione posthac eos esse
velitis, qui se pro salute vestra obtulerint invidiae periculis- 20
que omnibus: mihi quidem ipsi quid est, quod iam ad vitae
fructum possit adquiri, cum praesertim neque in honore
vestro neque in gloria virtutis quidquam videam altius, quo
mihi libeat adscendere? 29. Illud perficiam profecto,
Quirites, ut ea, quae gessi in consulatu, privatus tuear atque 25
ornem, ut, si qua est invidia in conservanda re publica
suscepta, laedat invidos, mihi valeat ad gloriam. Denique
ita me in re publica tractabo, ut meminerim semper quae
gesserim, curemque ut ea virtute, non casu gesta esse
videantur.   30

*Make your prayers, then, to Jupiter, and guard your homes to-night;
the danger will soon be over.*

Vos, Quirites, quoniam iam est nox, venerati Iovem
illum, custodem huius urbis ac vestrum, in vestra tecta
discedite et ea, quamquam iam est periculum depulsum,
tamen aeque ac priore nocte custodiis vigiliisque defendite.
Id ne vobis diutius faciendum sit atque ut in perpetua 35
pace esse possitis providebo.

M. TULLI CICERONIS
IN CATILINAM ORATIO QUARTA
HABITA IN SENATU.

I.

I thank you, Senators, for your anxiety on my behalf, but dismiss all care for me from your minds.

Video, patres conscripti, in me omnium vestrum ora atque oculos esse conversos; video vos non solum de vestro ac rei publicae, verum etiam, si id depulsum sit, de meo periculo esse sollicitos. Est mihi iucunda in malis et grata in dolore vestra erga me voluntas, sed eam, per deos 5 immortales, deponite atque obliti salutis meae de vobis ac de vestris liberis cogitate. Mihi si haec condicio consulatus data est, ut omnes acerbitates, omnes dolores cruciatusque perferrem, feram non solum fortiter, verum etiam libenter, dum modo meis laboribus vobis populoque Romano dignitas 10 salusque pariatur.

Come what may, I rejoice that I as consul have saved Rome.

2. Ego sum ille consul, patres conscripti, cui non forum, in quo omnis aequitas continetur, non campus, consularibus auspiciis consecratus, non curia, summum auxilium omnium gentium, non domus, commune perfugium, non lectus, ad 15 quietem datus, non denique haec sedes honoris umquam vacua mortis periculo atque insidiis fuit. Ego multa tacui, multa pertuli, multa concessi, multa meo quodam dolore in vestro timore sanavi. Nunc si hunc exitum consulatus mei di immortales esse voluerunt, ut vos populumque 20 Romanum ex caede miserrima, coniuges liberosque vestros virginesque Vestales ex acerbissima vexatione, templa atque delubra, hanc pulcherrimam patriam omnium nostrum ex foedissima flamma, totam Italiam ex bello et

60

vastitate eriperem, quaecumque mihi uni proponetur 25
fortuna, subeatur. Etenim si P. Lentulus suum nomen
inductus a vatibus fatale ad perniciem rei publicae fore
putavit, cur ego non laeter meum consulatum ad salutem
populi Romani prope fatalem exstitisse ?

II.

*I do not fear death with honour, so long as you and my dear ones are
saved.*

3. Quare, patres conscripti, consulite vobis, prospicite
patriae, conservate vos, coniuges, liberos fortunasque
vestras, populi Romani nomen salutemque defendite: mihi
parcere ac de me cogitare desinite. Nam primum debeo
sperare, omnes deos, qui huic urbi praesident, pro eo mihi 5
ac mereor relaturos esse gratiam: deinde, si quid obtigerit,
aequo animo paratoque moriar. Nam neque turpis mors
forti viro potest accidere neque immatura consulari nec
misera sapienti. Nec tamen ego sum ille ferreus, qui
fratris carissimi atque amantissimi praesentis maerore non 10
movear horumque omnium lacrimis, a quibus me circum-
sessum videtis. Neque meam mentem non domum saepe
revocat exanimata uxor et abiecta metu filia et parvulus
filius, quem mihi videtur amplecti res publica tamquam
obsidem consulatus mei, neque ille, qui exspectans huius 15
exitum diei stat in conspectu meo, gener. Moveor his
rebus omnibus, sed in eam partem, uti salvi sint vobiscum,
omnes, etiam si me vis aliqua oppresserit, potius, quam
et illi et nos una rei publicae peste pereamus.

*Think rather of the safety of the State, which is now menaced with
fire and sword.*

4. Quare, patres conscripti, incumbite ad salutem rei 20
publicae, circumspicite omnes procellas, quae impendent,
nisi providetis. Non Ti. Gracchus, quod iterum tribunus
plebis fieri voluit, non C. Gracchus, quod agrarios concitare
conatus est, non L. Saturninus, quod C. Memmium occidit,
in discrimen aliquod atque in vestrae severitatis iudicium 25
adducitur: tenentur ii, qui ad urbis incendium, ad vestram

omnium caedem, ad Catilinam accipiendum Romae restiterunt; tenentur litterae, signa, manus, denique unius
cuiusque confessio; sollicitantur Allobroges, servitia
excitantur, Catilina accersitur, id est initum consilium, 30
ut interfectis omnibus nemo ne ad deplorandum quidem
populi Romani nomen atque ad lamentandam tanti imperii
calamitatem relinquatur.

III.

*You have already shown by your actions that you are convinced of
the guilt of the conspirators.*

5. Haec omnia indices detulerunt, rei confessi sunt, vos
multis iam iudiciis iudicavistis, primum quod mihi gratias
egistis singularibus verbis et mea virtute atque diligentia
perditorum hominum coniurationem patefactam esse decrevistis, deinde quod P. Lentulum se abdicare praetura 5
coëgistis, tum quod eum et ceteros, de quibus iudicastis, in
custodiam dandos censuistis, maximeque quod meo nomine
supplicationem decrevistis, qui honos togato habitus ante
me est nemini; postremo hesterno die praemia legatis
Allobrogum Titoque Volturcio dedistis amplissima. Quae 10
sunt omnia eius modi, ut ii, qui in custodiam nominatim
dati sunt, sine ulla dubitatione a vobis damnati esse
videantur.

*Moreover, it is my duty as consul to warn you that there is no time to
lose; for the conspiracy is more widespread than men think.*

6. Sed ego institui referre ad vos, patres conscripti, tamquam integrum, et de facto quid iudicetis et de poena 15
quid censeatis. Illa praedicam, quae sunt consulis. Ego
magnum in re publica versari fuorem et nova quaedam
misceri et concitari mala iam pridem videbam, sed hanc
tantam, tam exitiosam haberi coniurationem a civibus
numquam putavi. Nunc quidquid est, quocumque vestrae 20
mentes inclinant atque sententiae, statuendum vobis ante
noctem est. Quantum facinus ad vos delatum sit, videtis.

Huic si paucos putatis adfines esse, vehementer erratis.
Latius opinione disseminatum est hoc malum: manavit
non solum per Italiam, verum etiam transcendit Alpes et 25
obscure serpens multas iam provincias occupavit. Id
opprimi sustentando aut prolatando nullo pacto potest:
quacumque ratione placet, celeriter vobis vindicandum est.

IV.

*Two proposals are before us. D. Silanus would put the prisoners to
death; C. Caesar would imprison them for life in some municipium.*

7. Video duas adhuc esse sententias, unam D. Silani, qui
censet eos, qui haec delere conati sunt, morte esse mul-
tandos, alteram C. Caesaris, qui mortis poenam removet,
ceterorum suppliciorum omnes acerbitates amplectitur.
Uterque et pro sua dignitate et pro rerum magnitudine in 5
summa severitate versatur. Alter eos, qui nos omnes vita
privare conati sunt, qui delere imperium, qui populi
Romani nomen exstinguere, punctum temporis frui vita et
hoc communi spiritu non putat oportere, atque hoc genus
poenae saepe in improbos cives in hac re publica esse 10
usurpatum recordatur. Alter intellegit mortem a dis
immortalibus non esse supplicii causa constitutam, sed aut
necessitatem naturae aut laborum ac miseriarum quietem.
Itaque eam sapientes numquam inviti, fortes saepe etiam
libenter oppetiverunt. Vincula vero et ea sempiterna 15
certe ad singularem poenam nefarii sceleris inventa sunt.
Municipiis dispertiri iubet.

*Caesar's proposal presents difficulties, but you can accept it if you
will. It certainly seems to be even more severe than the death penalty
itself.*

Habere videtur ista res iniquitatem, si imperare velis,
difficultatem, si rogare: decernatur tamen, si placet. 8.
Ego enim suscipiam, et, ut spero, reperiam, qui id, quod 20
salutis omnium causa statueritis, non putent esse suae
dignitatis recusare. Adiungit gravem poenam municipiis,
si quis eorum vincula ruperit: horribiles custodias circumdat

et dignas scelere hominum perditorum. Sancit, ne quis
eorum poenam, quos condemnat, aut per senatum aut per 25
populum levare possit: eripit etiam spem, quae sola homines
in miseriis consolari solet. Bona praeterea publicari iubet:
vitam solam relinquit nefariis hominibus, quam si eripuisset,
multas uno dolore animi atque corporis aerumnas et omnes
scelerum poenas ademisset. Itaque ut aliqua in vita 30
formido improbis esset posita, apud inferos eius modi quaedam illi antiqui supplicia impiis constituta esse voluerunt,
quod videlicet intellegebant his remotis non esse mortem
ipsam pertimescendam.

V.

*My personal interest is clear.   As Caesar is a popular leader, I shall
not, if you adopt his proposal, have so much cause to fear the attacks of
that party.*

9. Nunc, patres conscripti, ego mea video quid intersit.
Si eritis secuti sententiam C. Caesaris, quoniam hanc is in
re publica viam, quae popularis habetur, secutus est, fortasse minus erunt, hoc auctore et cognitore huiusce
sententiae, mihi populares impetus pertimescendi: sin 5
illam alteram, nescio an amplius mihi negotii contrahatur.
Sed tamen meorum periculorum rationes utilitas rei
publicae vincat. Habemus enim a Caesare, sicut ipsius
dignitas et maiorum eius amplitudo postulabat, sententiam
tamquam obsidem perpetuae in rem publicam voluntatis. 10
Intellectum est, quid interesset inter levitatem contionatorum et animum vere popularem, saluti populi con-
sulentem.

*Some of its members I see are absent, as though they refused to
recognise the Senate's right to judge this case.   Caesar, by his presence
here, shows that at least he does not question our jurisdiction.*

10. Video de istis, qui se populares haberi volunt,
abesse non neminem, ne de capite videlicet civium Roman- 15
orum sententiam ferat: is et nudius tertius in custodiam
cives Romanos dedit et supplicationem mihi decrevit et

indices hesterno die maximis praemiis adfecit Iam hoc
nemini dubium est, qui reo custodiam, quaesitori gratulationem, indici praemium decrerit, quid de tota re et causa 20
iudicarit.   At vero C. Caesar intellegit, legem Semproniam
esse de civibus Romanis constitutam, qui autem rei publicae
sit hostis, eum civem esse nullo modo posse; denique ipsum
latorem Semproniae legis iniussu populi poenas rei publicae
dependisse.   Idem ipsum Lentulum, largitorem et prodi- 25
gum, non putat, cum de pernicie populi Romani, exitio
huius urbis tam acerbe, tam crudeliter cogitarit, etiam
appellari posse popularem.   Itaque homo mitissimus atque
lenissimus non dubitat P. Lentulum aeternis tenebris vin-
culisque mandare et sancit in posterum, ne quis huius sup- 30
plicio levando se iactare et in perniciem populi Romani
posthac popularis esse possit: adiungit etiam publicationem
bonorum, ut omnes animi cruciatus et corporis etiam
egestas ac mendicitas consequatur.

VI.

*Whatever we decide we need not surely fear the charge of cruelty.   In
punishing crimes as terrible as these severity is the truest humanity.*

11. Quam ob rem sive hoc statueritis, dederitis mihi
comitem ad contionem populo carum atque iucundum, sive
Silani sententiam sequi malueritis, facile me atque vos
crudelitatis vituperatione populus Romanus exsolvet, atque
obtinebo eam multo leniorem fuisse.   Quamquam, patres 5
conscripti, quae potest esse in tanti sceleris immanitate
punienda crudelitas ? ego enim de meo sensu iudico.
Nam ita mihi salva re publica vobiscum perfrui liceat, ut
ego, quod in hac causa vehementior sum, non atrocitate
animi moveor—quis enim est me mitior ?—sed singu- 10
lari quadam humanitate et misericordia.   Videor enim
mihi videre hanc urbem, lucem orbis terrarum atque arcem
omnium gentium, subito uno incendio concidentem; cerno
animo sepulta in patria miseros atque insepultos acervos
civium; versatur mihi ante oculos adspectus Cethegi et 15
furor in vestra caede bacchantis.

Is it cruelty to deal harshly with those who with the aid of foreign enemies have planned to destroy Rome and massacre its inhabitants?

12. Cum vero mihi proposui regnantem Lentulum, sicut ipse se ex fatis sperasse confessus est, purpuratum esse huic Gabinium, cum exercitu venisse Catilinam, tum lamentationem matrum familias, tum fugam virginum 20 atque puerorum ac vexationem [virginum] Vestalium perhorresco, et quia mihi vehementer haec videntur misera atque miseranda, idcirco in eos, qui ea perficere voluerunt, me severum vehementemque praebeo. Etenim quaero, si quis pater familias, liberis suis a servo interfectis, uxore 25 occisa, incensa domo, supplicium de servo non quam acerbissimum sumpserit, utrum is clemens ac misericors an inhumanissimus et crudelissimus esse videatur ? Mihi vero importunus ac ferreus, qui non dolore et cruciatu nocentis suum dolorem cruciatumque lenierit. Sic nos in his homini- 30 bus, qui nos, qui coniuges, qui liberos nostros trucidare voluerunt, qui singulas unius cuiusque nostrum domos et hoc universum rei publicae domicilium delere conati sunt, qui id egerunt, ut gentem Allobrogum in vestigiis huius urbis atque in cinere deflagrati imperii collocarent, si vehe- 35 mentissimi fuerimus, misericordes habebimur: sin remissiores esse voluerimus, summae nobis crudelitatis in patriae civiumque pernicie fama subeunda est.

Remember what L. Caesar said yesterday; yet the offences of C. Gracchus cannot be compared to those of Catilina.

13. Nisi vero cuipiam L. Caesar, vir fortissimus et amantissimus rei publicae, crudelior nudius tertius visus 40 est, cum sororis suae, feminae lectissimae, virum praesentem et audientem vita privandum esse dixit, cum avum suum iussu consulis interfectum filiumque eius impuberem, legatum a patre missum, in carcere necatum esse dixit. Quorum quod simile factum ? quod initum delendae rei 45 publicae consilium ? Largitionis voluntas tum in re publica versata est et partium quaedam contentio. Atque illo tempore huius avus Lentuli, vir clarissimus, armatus Grac-

chum est persecutus. Ille etiam grave tum vulnus accepit,
ne quid de summa re publica deminueretur: hic ad ever- 50
tenda fundamenta rei publicae Gallos accersit, servitia con-
citat, Catilinam vocat, attribuit nos trucidandos Cethego et
ceteros cives interficiendos Gabinio, urbem inflammandam
Cassio, totam Italiam vastandam diripiendamque Catilinae.
Vereamini censeo, ne in hoc scelere tam immani ac nefando 55
nimis aliquid severe statuisse videamini: multo magis est
verendum, ne remissione poenae crudeles in patriam, quam
ne severitate animadversionis nimis vehementes in acerbis·
simos hostes fuisse videamur.

VII.

Do not fear that we shall lack strength to carry out our decision.
Every class in the State is with us.

14. Sed ea, quae exaudio, patres conscripti, dissimulare
non possum. Iaciuntur enim voces, quae perveniunt ad
aures meas, eorum qui vereri videntur, ut habeam satis
praesidii ad ea, quae vos statueritis hodierno die, transi-
gunda. Omnia et provisa et parata et constituta sunt, 5
patres conscripti, cum mea summa cura atque diligentia,
tum multo etiam maiore populi Romani ad summum
imperium retinendum et ad communes fortunas conser-
vandas voluntate. Omnes adsunt omnium ordinum
homines, omnium generum, omnium denique aetatum; 10
plenum est forum, plena templa circum forum, pleni omnes
aditus huius templi ac loci. Causa est enim post urbem
conditam haec inventa sola, in qua omnes sentirent unum
atque idem, praeter eos, qui cum sibi viderent esse pereun-
dum, cum omnibus potius quam soli perire voluerunt. 15

The Roman knights, after a disagreement lasting many years, are
now your firm allies; the acrarian tribunes, the government clerks, all
free-born citizens are eager to support you.

15. Hosce ego homines excipio et secerno libenter, neque
enim in improborum civium, sed in acerbissimorum hostium

numero habendos puto. Ceteri vero, di immortales, qua
frequentia, quo studio, qua virtute ad communem salutem
dignitatemque consentiunt! Quid ego equites Romanos 20
commemorem? qui vobis ita summam ordinis consiliique
concedunt, ut vobiscum de amore rei publicae certent;
quos ex multorum annorum dissensione huius ordinis ad
societatem concordiamque revocatos hodiernus dies vobiscum atque haec causa coniungit. Quam si coniunctionem, 25
in consulatu confirmatam meo, perpetuam in re publica
tenuerimus, confirmo vobis nullum posthac malum civile ac
domesticum ad ullam rei publicae partem esse venturum.
Pari studio defendendae rei publicae convenisse video
tribunos aerarios fortissimos viros; scribas item universos, 30
quos cum casu hic dies ad aerarium frequentasset, video ab
exspectatione sortis ad salutem communem esse conversos.
16. Omnis ingenuorum adest multitudo, etiam tenuissimo-
rum. Quis est enim, cui non haec templa, adspectus urbis,
possessio libertatis, lux denique haec ipsa et commune 35
patriae solum cum sit carum, tum vero dulce atque iucundum?

VIII.

*The freedmen, too, are enthusiastic in their country's cause, and even
the slaves contribute all they can.*

Operae pretium est, patres conscripti, libertinorum hominum studia cognoscere, qui sua virtute fortunam huius
civitatis consecuti hanc suam patriam iudicant, quam
quidam hic nati et summo nati loco non patriam suam, sed
urbem hostium esse iudicaverunt. Sed quid ego hosce 5
homines ordinesque commemoro, quos privatae fortunae,
quos communis res publica, quos denique libertas, ea quae
dulcissima est, ad salutem patriae defendendam excitavit?
Servus est nemo, qui modo tolerabili condicione sit servitutis, qui non audaciam civium perhorrescat, qui non haec 10
stare cupiat, qui non quantum audet et quantum potest,
conferat ad communem salutem voluntatis.

*Lentulus made an attempt to win over the shopkeepers, but in vain.
Their interests are bound up with the maintenance of order.*

17. Quare si quem vestrum forte commovet hoc, quod
auditum est, lenonem quendam Lentuli concursare circum
tabernas, pretio sperare sollicitari posse animos egentium 15
atque imperitorum, est id quidem coeptum atque tempta-
tum, sed nulli sunt inventi tam aut fortuna miseri aut
voluntate perditi, qui non illum ipsum sellae atque operis
et quaestus cotidiani locum, qui non cubile ac lectulum
suum, qui denique non cursum hunc otiosum vitae suae 20
salvum esse velint.   Multo vero maxima pars eorum, qui in
tabernis sunt, immo vero—id enim potius est dicendum—
genus hoc universum amantissimum est otii.   Etenim omne
instrumentum, omnis opera atque quaestus frequentia
civium sustentatur, alitur otio: quorum si quaestus occlusis 25
tabernis minui solet, quid tandem incensis futurum fuit ?

IX.

The people of Rome will not fail you ; do not fail them.

18. Quae cum ita sint, patres conscripti, vobis populi
Romani praesidia non desunt: vos ne populo Romano
deesse videamini providete.   Habetis consulem ex plurimis
periculis et insidiis atque ex media morte non ad vitam
suam, sed ad salutem vestram reservatum; omnes ordines 5
ad conservandam rem publicam mente, voluntate, voce
consentiunt; obsessa facibus et telis impiae coniurationis
vobis supplex manus tendit patria communis, vobis se,
vobis vitam omnium civium, vobis arcem et Capitolium,
vobis aras Penatium, vobis illum ignem Vestae sempiter- 10
num, vobis omnium deorum templa atque delubra, vobis
muros atque urbis tecta commendat.   Praeterea de vestra
vita, de coniugum vestrarum atque liberorum anima, de
fortunis omnium, de sedibus, de focis vestris hodierno die
vobis iudicandum est.   15

Take advantage of their unanimity and my devotion.   Think of the danger we have escaped and take measures against a renewal of such danger.

19. Habetis ducem memorem vestri, oblitum sui, quae non semper facultas datur; habetis omnes ordines, omnes homines, universum populum Romanum, id quod in civili causa hodierno die primum videmus, unum atque idem sentientem. Cogitate, quantis laboribus fundatum im- 20 perium, quanta virtute stabilitam libertatem, quanta deorum benignitate auctas exaggeratasque fortunas una nox paene delerit. Id ne unquam posthac non modo confici, sed ne cogitari quidem possit a civibus, hodierno die providendum est. Atque haec, non ut vos, qui mihi 25 studio paene praecurritis, excitarem, locutus sum, sed ut mea vox, quae debet esse in re publica princeps, officio functa consulari videretur.

X.

I well know the dangers that threaten me, but I shall never repent of what I have done.

20. Nunc antequam ad sententiam redeo, de me pauca dicam. Ego, quanta manus est coniuratorum, quam videtis esse permagnam, tantam me inimicorum multitudinem suscepisse video, sed eam esse iudico turpem et infirmam et abiectam. Quodsi aliquando alicuius furore 5 et scelere concitata manus ista plus valuerit quam vestra ac rei publicae dignitas, me tamen meorum factorum atque consiliorum numquam, patres conscripti, paenitebit. Etenim mors, quam illi mihi fortasse minitantur, omnibus est parata: vitae tantam laudem, quanta vos me vestris 10 decretis honestastis, nemo est adsecutus; ceteris enim bene gestae, mihi uni conservatae rei publicae gratulationem decrevistis.

My name will be inscribed on the roll of fame with Scipio, Marius, and Pompeius.

21. Sit Scipio clarus ille, cuius consilio atque virtute Hannibal in Africam redire atque Italia decedere coactus 15

est; ornetur alter eximia laude Africanus, qui duas urbes
huic imperio infestissimas, Carthaginem Numantiamque,
delevit; habeatur vir egregius Paulus ille, cuius currum rex
potentissimus quondam et nobilissimus Perses honestavit;
sit aeterna gloria Marius, qui bis Italiam obsidione et metu 20
servitutis liberavit; anteponatur omnibus Pompeius, cuius
res gestae atque virtutes isdem quibus solis cursus regionibus
ac terminis continentur; erit profecto inter horum laudes
aliquid loci nostrae gloriae, nisi forte maius est patefacere
nobis provincias, quo exire possimus, quam curare ut etiam 25
illi, qui absunt, habeant quo victores revertantur.

*My enemies in Rome will wage eternal war on me; but I trust in the
protection of all honest citizens.*

22. Quamquam est uno loco condicio melior externae
victoriae quam domesticae, quod hostes alienigenae aut
oppressi serviunt aut recepti beneficio se obligatos putant;
qui autem ex numero civium, dementia aliqua depravati, 30
hostes patriae semel esse coeperunt, eos cum a pernicie rei
publicae reppuleris, nec vi coërcere nec beneficio placare
possis. Quare mihi cum perditis civibus aeternum bellum
susceptum esse video. Id ego vestro bonorumque omnium
auxilio memoriaque tantorum periculorum, quae non modo 35
in hoc populo, qui servatus est, sed in omnium gentium
sermonibus ac mentibus semper haerebit, a me atque a
meis facile propulsari posse confido. Neque ulla profecto
tanta vis reperietur, quae coniunctionem vestram equitum-
que Romanorum et tantam conspirationem bonorum 40
omnium confringere et labefactare possit.

XI.

*One reward I ask, your remembrance of my exertions and my sacrifices,
and your protection for my son. Vote, then, bravely, remembering what
is at stake, and I will carry out your decision.*

23. Quae cum ita sint, pro imperio, pro exercitu, pro
provincia, quam neglexi, pro triumpho ceterisque laudis
insignibus, quae sunt a me propter urbis vestraeque salutis

custodiam repudiata, pro clientelis hospitiisque provincialibus, quae tamen urbanis opibus non minore labore 5
tueor quam comparo, pro his igitur omnibus rebus, et pro
meis in vos singularibus studiis proque hac, quam per-
spicitis, ad conservandam rem publicam diligentia nihil
a vobis nisi huius temporis totiusque mei consulatus
memoriam postulo: quae dum erit in vestris fixa mentibus, 10
tutissimo me muro saeptum esse arbitrabor. Quodsi meam
spem vis improborum fefellerit atque superaverit, com-
mendo vobis parvum meum filium, cui profecto satis erit
praesidii non solum ad salutem, verum etiam ad dignitatem,
si eius, qui haec omnia suo solius periculo conservarit, illum 15
filium esse memineritis. Quapropter de summa salute
vestra populique Romani, de vestris coniugibus ac liberis,
de aris ac focis, de fanis atque templis, de totius urbis tectis
ac sedibus, de imperio ac libertate, de salute Italiae, de
universa re publica decernite diligenter, ut instituistis, ac 20
fortiter. Habetis eum consulem, qui et parere vestris
decretis non dubitet et ea, quae statueritis quoad vivet,
defendere et per se ipsum praestare.

NOTES.

N.B.—The references are to chapters and lines. Proper names will be found in the Index, and are also occasionally mentioned in the Notes.

An obelus (†) prefixed to a word denotes that the text is doubtful. The letters *v.l.* = *varia lectio* = variant reading.

FIRST SPEECH.

Ch. I. Consult the Index for Ahala, Ti. Gracchus, Maelius, Palatium, Scipio.

1. quo usque: this is often written in one word, *quousque*; like *respublica, quamdiu, senatusconsultum*, etc.

tandem: " I pray "; a rhetorical use of the word, common in questions.

abutere: fut. simple (*abutēre*), as shown by the parallel verbs *eludet, iactabit.*

2. quam diu etiam: *etiam* modifies *diu*; " how long yet ? " *i.e.* " how much longer ? " Cp. *vixdum etiam* in iv. 24.

†nos eludet: many omit the word *nos*, as it does not occur in a quotation which a later writer makes from the speech; but *eludet* seems used in its transitive sense. It would be easy, however, to understand as object *patientiam nostram*, from the preceding sentence.

3. nihil . . . moverunt: the repeated *nihil* is used adverbially with *moverunt.* This repetition of a word at the beginning of successive clauses for rhetorical effect is not infrequent, and is called *anaphora* or *repetitio.*

4. praesidium Palatii: Cicero enumerates the things Catilina must have seen on his way to the senate. For *Palatium* see Index of Proper Names.

5. consursus bonorum: Cicero's partisans, many of them in arms, were at hand to support him. By *boni* he generally means his own party, the *optimates* or aristocrats. The opposition were *improbi.*

6. senatus locus: *senatus* often means a " meeting of the senate." The place was the temple of Jupiter Stator, on the northern slope of the guarded Palatium; not the usual *curia* in the Forum.

7. constrictam: to be taken predicatively with *teneri.*

9. quid proxima . . . arbitraris: see Introduction, §§ 3 and 6. Note that *quid, ubi, quos* introduce indirect questions (with the subjunctive) depending on the direct question *quem arbitraris.*

10. quid consilii: partitive genitive, as also *nostrum* following.

73

13. immo vero: "nay rather," used to correct an incorrect or inadequate expression.

17. vitemus: the subjunctive is due, not to the hypothetical form of the sentence, but to the fact of its being a " reported condition," an indirect (oblique) form, introduced by *videmur* (" we seem to ourselves," *i.e.* " we think "); the direct form would be *satisfacimus . . . si vitamus.*

18. duci . . . oportebat: note the Latin present infinitive with " auxiliaries of mood " (*possum, volo, debeo*, etc.), where English has the perfect infinitive. But see below, ii. 26, note on *factum esse oportuit.*

19. an vero: the interrogative particle *an* introduces the second half of a double question; but often (as here) the first half is only implied in the context. " Catilina ought to have been put to death, ought he not ? Or ought we to put up with him, though we have the precedent of Scipio killing Gracchus ? " The two questions that are expressed (after *an*) are co-ordinated for rhetorical effect; though logically a subordinate clause is required in place of the first, as in the above paraphrase.

21. privatus: not a *magistratus*, as the pontificate was permanent; moreover, Scipio was not pontiff at the time referred to.

23. nam illa . . . praetereo: the *nam* explains some minor unexpressed idea that would naturally be in the mind of speaker and audience. " I quote the case of Gracchus only, *for* there is no need to go into ancient history."

24. quod . . . occidit: the beginner must notice that *quod* with the indicative is often to be translated " the fact that," not " because." The clause is thus a substantival clause that may be a subject or object of the main verb; here it is in partitive apposition to *illa antiqua*, and so object of *praetereo.*

25. fuit: the perfect sometimes rhetorically implies " has been, but is no longer." Cp. *Troia fuit*, " Troy is no more."

26. ista: this pronoun, like *is*, is sometimes used in the sense of *talis.*

ut . . . coercerent: consecutive subjunctive, denoting a result.

28. senatus consultum: the *consultum* (or *decretum*) *ultimum.* See Introduction, § 6 (October 21st). The formula is quoted below at the beginning of Ch. II.

29. consilium . . . auctoritas: to be taken closely together; the deliberative and authorising functions of the senate had been duly discharged; but the consuls, the executive, failed the state in the hour of her need. Note the various senses of *consilium*: (*a*) l. 10, a plan, scheme; (*b*) l. 29. advice, counsel; (*c*) sometimes, a council, deliberative assembly. *Concilium* is used only in the concrete sense of " a meeting."

Ch. II. Consult the Index for Etruria, Fulvius, C. Gracchus, Marius, Opimius, Saturninus, Servilius, Valerius.

1. **L. Opimius consul:** only one consul is mentioned in this *decretum ultimum*, as the other was away on service in Gallia Narbonensis.

2. **detrimenti:** partitive genitive dependent on *quid*.

3. **intercessit; interfectus est:** another instance of the co-ordination of clauses (instead of subordination) for rhetorical effect. We should say "Before a single night passed, Gaius Gracchus was killed."

quasdam seditionum suspiciones: the offences of the Gracchi were really grave in Cicero's eyes; but here, as above, he uses mild expressions to strengthen his argument. The force of the indefinite *quasdam* is to weaken *suspiciones*: "some vague suspicion." Cp. note on *non mentem aliquam*, vi. 25. The word *seditio* means literally "a going apart"—hence political schism or insurrection; it was generally applied to the proceedings of the plebeian and democratic parties.

4. **clarissimo . . . maioribus:** "a man of brilliant ancestry" (ablative of description), or "though his ancestors were highly distinguished" (ablative of attendant circumstances). Or the case may be classed as ablative of origin—"sprung from."

7. **num unum diem . . . remorata est:** lit. "did it keep them waiting a single day?" Render, "did it grant them a single day's respite?"

8. **mors ac reipublicae poena:** this may be regarded as hendiadys, *i.e.* a form of expression in which two coupled substantives are used to express one idea with some amplification. The conjunction is often intensive rather than connective. Cp. Vergil's well-known *pateris libamus et auro*, "we pour libations from bowls, e'en bowls of gold." The text, freely translated, means, "death,—aye, and the death that came as the avenging punishment of the state which they outraged." Death is strongly personified, and gives a personal notion also to *rei publicae* and *poena*; the latter often meaning the spirit of punishment; and *Poenae* = the Furies.

9. **at vero nos:** *nos* is strongly contrasted with the previously mentioned consuls. *Vero,* besides giving emphasis, is often strongly adversative, like *verum*.

vicesimum iam diem: a slight exaggeration, as by the Roman inclusive method of reckoning it was only nineteen days from October 21st, when the decree was passed. See Introduction, § 3.

10. **horum:** Cicero points to the assembled senators.

12. **tabulis:** the minutes, etc., of business in the senate stored away somewhere with other public documents and archives.

in vagina: the metaphor introduced by the word *aciem* ("edge") above is here kept up.

13. convēnit: impersonal, " it was fitting."

15. patres conscripti: the usual formula in addressing the senate. It is generally explained as follows: In early Rome the original senators were *patres* or patricians; but their numbers dwindled for various reasons, and after the expulsion of the Kings it was found expedient to add a number of new senators from the highest plebeians; and these, not being *patres,* were called " enrolled " members or *conscripti.* The whole body (300 members) was then called *patres conscripti,* "fathers and enrolled senators." The omission of *et* in semi-technical or legal expressions is common; *e.g.* in dating a year by the names of the consuls, *A. Virginio, T. Vetusio consulibus.* Another explanation is that the phrase means simply " enrolled fathers," *i.e.* those *patres* or patricians who were made members of the senate.

me esse clementem: the usual construction with *cupio* would be *clemens esse.*

17. inertiae nequitiaeque condemno: the objective genitive with a verb of condemning usually expresses the charge, sometimes the penalty.

18. in Etruriae faucibus: *i.e.* over a gorge in the W. Apennines near Faesulae. The ablative singular *fauce* is sometimes used by poets; otherwise the word is plural.

19. crescit in dies singulos: " grows every day." Where a daily increase or decrease is marked, *indies,* or a phrase like the text, is used for " daily "; whereas the mere repetition of an act is expressed by *cotidie,* as at the end of this sentence.

21. atque adeo: *adeo* is here intensive, " and even."

23. credo, erit verendum mihi, ne non potius: *credo* marks as usual the irony of the expression. Cicero's real meaning was *erit verendum ne potius :* " I shall have to fear the charge of dilatoriness rather than that of cruelty." Note the construction is *verendum ne non*; the *vereor ut* construction, which is identical in meaning, is less common. Note also the contrast between *omnes boni,* " all good patriots," and *quisquam,* " one single individual of any kind." For this use of *quisquam* cp. l. 30 below.

24. serius: " too late." When no standard of comparison is expressed, the comparative degree of adjectives and adverbs often means " more (than is proper)."

26. iam pridem factum esse oportuit: the use of the perfect infinitive with the modal auxiliary *oportuit* seems to contradict the principle noticed above (see note on *duci oportebat,* i. 17). And in ii. 13 we have had *te interfectum esse convenit.* In both instances, however, the perfect infinitive is used to lay stress on the completion of the action. Such uses are exceptional and uncommon.

27. tum denique: like *tum demum,* " then, and not till then."

29. inveniri poterit: the future-perfect would have been the regular tense here, as *si te iussero* above, l. 23; but with modal auxiliaries like *possum*, etc., some freedom is allowed in the tense, and even the mood, usage.

qui id non iure . . . fateatur: after *nemo* and other such negatives we often have *quin* for *qui non*; but Cicero is distinctly fond of the latter form, of course with the subjunctive, which is consecutive. It is only after a negative or interrogative principal sentence that *qui* can take the place of *ut* corresponding to *tam*. *Iure* is one of the ablatives of manner which has practically passed into an adverb, and consequently need not be accompanied by the preposition *cum* or an adjective. So its opposite *iniuriā*, vii. 15.

30. quam diu quisquam erit: *quisquam* thus used in a sentence that has no negative or comparative denotes the barest possible minimum (" one single man "), or the closest approximation to the negative. The simple future *erit* is quite correct here because the time it denotes is strictly coincident or commensurate with the time of the principal verb *vives*.

qui . . . audeat: consecutive subjunctive, as *fateatur* in the line above. *Qui* may be regarded as equivalent to *talis ut is*; and the term " generic " subjunctive is often applied to this usage.

32. †obsessus: *v.l. oppressus,* " crushed down."

Ch. III. Consult the Index for Manlius, Praeneste.

1. etenim: " for indeed ": the *et* is intensive, while *enim* is explanatory of the sentence above beginning *vives, sed vives* (ii. 30).

quod expectes: the consecutive subjunctive again following a relative.

2. †coetus nefarios: *v.l. coeptus* in many MSS. would mean " undertakings "; but the word is very rare, and hardly legitimate.

3. parietibus: the walls of a house, as distinct from the city walls *(moenia)*; while *murus* is a term of general application. *Paries* may be a " party-wall," but the derivation from *pars, partis,* is incorrect.

voces coniurationis tuae: the *coniuratio* of Catilina may be here personified; but more probably the word is used as practically the equivalent of *coniuratores;* just as *latrocinium = latrones,* and *servitium* often means " slaves " as a class.

5. obliviscere: distinguish carefully between *obliviscĕre* (as here) and *obliviscēre.*

6. tĕnērĭs: distinguish from *tĕnĕrĭs,* the dative or ablative plural of the adjective *tener.*

7. licet recognoscas: the latter word may be called a jussive subjunctive in quasi-dependence on *licet.* The construction *licet ut* is considerably less common, and it is not sufficient to explain such subjunctives as *recognoscas* here by saying *ut* is omitted. Such

expressions were without doubt regarded as two independent verbs in an early stage of the language. " Go over these with me: you may " would be the original meaning; cp. the expression Cicero has just used, *Muta istam mentem, mihi crede.* The natural tendency of language would be to make the two verbs combine into one complex sentence; but it is impossible in many cases to say how far the tendency has gone.

meministine me ... dicere: the present infinitive (for a past event) is constantly found after *memini* to denote the direct memory of an eye-witness. Catilina is supposed still to have the scene before his mind's eye.

9. qui dies futurus esset: the repetition of the word *dies* makes the language more formal and impressive. *Futurus esset* is the proper indirect (oblique) form to represent Cicero's *oratio recta,* which would be *qui dies erit.*

10. satellitem atque administrum: Cicero is fond of explaining or amplifying his meaning by adding a synonym. The term *satelles* is used as an invidious one, suggesting the creatures of an Eastern potentate.

15. tum cum . . . profugerunt: *cum* followed by the indicative must be strictly temporal; though it is incorrect to suppose that *cum* with the subjunctive cannot denote time, as (with imperfect and pluperfect subjunctive) it often marks the temporal sequence of different events, and may be translated " after "; cp. vi. 10. *Cum* with a past tense of the indicative generally denotes (1) a precise point of time, often made definite by an expressed antecedent: as here *tum cum,* and *illo die cum* in the next sentence. The *cum* clause is thus exactly the same as an ordinary relative clause with the indicative. (2) It sometimes denotes repeated action or " indefinite frequency "; e.g. *Cum rosam viderat, tum incipere ver arbitrabatur* (Cic. *Verr.* 5, 10), " Whenever he saw the rose, he used to think spring was beginning." Cp. xiii. 8, *cum ... iactantur, si ... biberunt,* and note thereon. After Cicero's time the later writers began to use the subjunctive in this frequentative sense.

16. sui conservandi: *sui* is in origin the genitive singular neuter of the possessive adjective *suus*; and though it is used as the genitive of *se* with singular or plural meaning indifferently, a gerundive accompanying it is always singular.

20. nostra tamen qui remansissemus caede: a possessive adjective implies a genitive pronoun; and here the relative *qui* agrees with the antecedent (" of us," objective genitive implied in *nostrā*. So we find in Ovid *nostros flentis ocellos*: " the eyes of me weeping "; where *nostros = meos = mei* (possessive genitive). Cp. iv. 11, *nostro omnium interitu.* The subjunctive *remansissemus* is used because the clause is a " reported definition," *i.e.* a definition quoted from Catilina's words, *eorum qui remanserunt caede contentus sum.*

22. **quid:** in rhetorical style this often becomes a mere particle marking transition, "again"; but it is always followed by a question.

Praeneste: see Index. Its occupation would have given Catilina a stronghold commanding a large part of Latium.

25. †**quod non . . . audiam:** *v.l. quin* for *quod non*. The subjunctive is consecutive, as before explained. The negative runs on to *videam* and *sentiam*.

Ch. IV. Consult the Index for Laeca.

1. **tandem:** the word has not here the strong rhetorical force it has in questions (see the first sentence of the speech). It is used with very much the same force, almost colloquial, as *modo* with imperatives. The connection of thought runs thus: "I am fully acquainted with everything you do. *Just let me recount* to you your quite recent proceedings; and you will see the truth of this assertion." It must be remembered that the division of the speech into chapters is quite arbitrary, and does not necessarily denote pauses in thought.

noctem illam superiorem: the phrase seems a repetition or quotation of *superiore nocte* in i. 9. "The night before last" would be that of November 6th. See Introduction, § 6.

2. **iam intelliges:** the English idiom generally requires the conjunction " and " to connect an imperative and the future that denotes the result of carrying out the command; but Cicero never uses a conjunction.

3. **priore nocte:** apparently the same as *superiore nocte.*

4. **inter falcarios:** "in the scythe-makers' quarter." So "*inter lignarios*" (Joiners'-street) in Livy, xxxv. 41.

5. **amentiae scelerisque:** this is practically hendiadys—" criminal madness," or " mad crime."

6. **convincam, si negas:** *convincam* is the future simple indicative, not a subjunctive, which normally would require *neges.* The future perfect (*negaveris*), usually forming the protasis to a simple future, would not be right here; for the present *negas* means " if you are now denying it by your silence, I shall still convict you out of the mouths of others."

8. **ubinam gentium:** so we find *ubi terrarum.* The partitive genitive in these cases depends on an adverb; *ubi =* " in what part ? " Cp. *id temporis* below, iv. 28. *Nam*, when attached as an enclitic to an interrogative pronoun or adverb, signifies surprise or emotion in the person who puts the question (like the Greek γάρ).

10. **orbis terrae:** *terra* is generally " a country," or " dry land " as opposed to sea. The Greek mathematicians were aware that the earth is a sphere.

11. de nostro omnium interitu: compare *nostra, qui remansissemus, caede,* and the note thereon above, iii. 20. Also *parens omnium nostrum* and note, vii. 24.

13. cogitent: the phrase *sunt . . . qui . . . cogitent* is a common type of the phrase of the consecutive subjunctive sometimes called " generic," and already noted several times. In poetry an indicative would sometimes be found; but in correct prose *sunt qui cogitant* should refer, not to a class of men who are wont to plot, but to specific individuals who actually are plotting.

hos . . . de re publica sententiam rogo: the phrase *aliquem sententiam rogare,* " to question a member about his views on a motion," is a technical or (as we should say) parliamentary expression (cp. viii. 19, note). Apart from it the verb *rogo,* in the sense of " to enquire," must not be used with two accusatives, unless one is a neuter adjective or pronoun, as these latter approximate to adverbs. Thus, of the two accusatives one is an adverbial usage (and consequently may go with the passive voice), the other is the direct object of the verb and must be the subject of the passive verb; the former is the " internal," the latter is the " external " object. *Hos sententiam rogo* transposed is *Hi sententiam a me rogantur.*

15. nondum voce vulnero: he did not name or specifically accuse them.

16. fuisti igitur: *igitur* resumes the train of argument interrupted by *O di immortales* and what follows.

17. statuisti . . . placeret: note the difference. *Statuo* is used here of the expression of the resolve in words, *placet* of the resolve as formed in the mind. With *placeret* supply *tibi.*

quo quemque: *quisque* is regarded almost as an enclitic, and immediately follows (1) a superlative or ordinal numeral, as *optimus quisque,* " all the best men "; (2) the reflexives *se, suus,* etc., as *pro se quisque,* " every man for himself "; this is the most distinctly " distributive " use; (3) a relative or interrogative form (including adverbs), as in the text; in this idiom the pronoun is often indefinite (and confused with *quis* or *aliquis*) rather than distributive.

18. quos relinqueres: *quos = ut eos;* the subjunctive is mainly final (denoting purpose), though the consecutive idea may be faintly seen.

19. discripsisti: distinguish this verb from *describo,* which does not imply division.

21. quod ego viverem: the subjunctive because the reason is reported as Catilina's statement.

duo equites: said to be C. Cornelius and L. Vargunteius. The *equites* were the second *ordo* or grade in Roman society, coming after the senators. The property qualification of an *eques* was fixed by Augustus at 400,000 sesterces: its amount before his time is not known. They were so called because in early times, when society was organised on a purely military basis, they served as cavalry. Now they formed the mercantile and monied class, including nearly all the *publicani* or tax-farmers. As a body they strongly supported Cicero, who sprang from their ranks.

22. qui liberarent: consecutive subjunctive.

23. vixdum etiam: connect these words, and cp. *quam diu etiam* in i. 2.

26. salutatum: supine with a verb of motion. The early morning visit to men of position and *patroni* was a very common custom at Rome.

27. multis ac summis: the Latin idiom requires the conjunction between adjectives (and adverbs), denoting different ideas.

28. id temporis: "at that point of time": *id* must be considered an adverbial accusative, and *temporis* a partitive genitive. Cp. *ubinam gentium* above, iv. 8, and the similar phrase *id aetatis,* " at that time of life." As, however, there is a decided tendency for neuter forms to approximate to indeclinables, the distinct case-notion may have faded out of the *id*.

Ch. V. Consult the Index for Iuppiter Stator.

3. **Manliana castra:** the camp in Etruria commanded by Manlius. The Latin language is very free in its manufacture and use of adjectives derived from proper names.

desiderant: the verb *desidero* means, not " to desire," but to " feel the loss " of anything, to " miss " it.

4. si minus: *i.e.* " if not all." *Minus* is often practically equivalent to *non*.

9. antiquissimo custodi: see Index *s.v.* Iuppiter.

gratia: in the singular the feeling of " gratitude "; whereas *gratiae* (plural) is the outward expression of the feeling, or " thanks," as in *agere gratias,* " to return thanks."

11. in uno homine: " in the person of one man," *i.e.* Cicero himself. Others make it refer to Catilina, the sentence then meaning " the fate of the state in supreme crises must not depend on, *i.e.* be settled by, a single man." But Cicero in this chapter is dwelling on the danger from the other conspirators, and he may always be trusted to talk about himself where possible.

15. in campo: the *Campus Martius* was the usual meeting-place of the *Comitia Centuriata,* which elected consuls. Being theoretically the army of the state, it could not meet within the city. The election in question was for the consuls for 62. Of the *competitores,* D. Iunius Silanus and L. Licinius Murena were chosen.

17. nullo tumultu publice concitato: technically the word *tumultus* was used for any appeal to arms or armed rising in Italy, as opposed to *bellum,* a war with foreigners abroad.

24. **huius imperii:** *i.e.* his consular authority enlarged by the extraordinary powers conferred on him by the *consultum ultimum.*

25. **disciplinaeque maiorum:** the reference is to the historical precedents (mentioned in Ch. I. and II.), that would warrant the summary execution of Catilina.

26. **ad severitatem:** " in the matter of " or " on the score of severity."

27. **residebit:** a strong metaphor (" will settle down like dregs "), which is carried on in *exhaurietur* and *sentina.*

29. **iam dudum hortor:** " I have long been urging." The present indicative with *iam dudum* denotes an action that has been going on for some time.

tuorum comitum . . . sentina rei publicae: *sentina* is the bilge of a ship, or a drain of any kind : then the refuse or dregs that collect there. Take *sentina rei publicae* as one notion (" political garbage "), on which depends the genitive *tuorum comitum* (" consisting of your companions "), which may be classed as a genitive of definition or material.

32. **tua sponte:** in prose of the best period *sponte* (ablative of manner) is always accompanied by a possessive adjective.

faciebas: the imperfect used of a contemplated action: " you were on the point of doing."

hostem: Catilina had been publicly pronounced a *hostis patriae.*

33. **num in exsilium:** Catilina is supposed to ask this question. Cicero does not order Catilina into exile, but advises him to go, because exile was not a legally recognised punishment that could be inflicted; it was rather a means, voluntarily adopted, of anticipating and avoiding the extreme penalties of law. It appears from a passage in Sallust that a Roman had a legal right thus to avoid punishment.

Ch. VI. Consult the Index for Lepidus, Tullus.

1. **quod . . . possit:** consecutive subjective, the relative *quod* being as usual equivalent to *(tale) ut id.*

2. **in qua . . . est:** the relative here is (as often) little more than a co-ordinating conjunction, and may be resolved into *nam in ea.*

nemo est . . . qui te non metuat: as has been noted above (ii. 29), Cicero seems to prefer *qui non* to *quin* in these negative clauses containing consecutive subjunctives.

4. **domesticae turpitudinis:** *i.e.* family scandals; while *privatarum rerum dedecus* refers to his private life outside his family circle.

7. **adulescentulo:** the diminutive form expresses here half pity, half contempt. Cicero, however, often uses the word without any such notion; and it applies even to men of twenty or thirty years of age.

8. irretisses: this may be called the consecutive (or "generic") subjunctive, as no individual is referred to, but only the type of a class. Or *quem* may be regarded as equivalent to *cum eum*: " after you had ensnared him."

9. ad audaciam: "for deeds of violence"; or perhaps "to make him bold." The elaborate care with which Cicero balances his rhetorical antitheses often tends to obscure the meaning. Cp. v. 26, *ad severitatem lenius.*

facem praetulisti: the metaphor is from the Roman custom of being lighted home by a slave with a torch at night. There may be also in the metaphor the idea of lighting up the fires of passion.

10. quid vero: the expression marks emphatically the transition to a new instance of Catilina's depravity.

11. alio incredibili scelere: Sallust says he put his son to death to oblige Orestilla, the profligate woman he wished to marry.

13. tanti facinoris immanitas: *i.e.* "crime of such enormity." Cicero generally uses *facinus* in a bad sense.

14. aut non vindicata esse: understand *si exstiterit.* No one had come forward to prosecute Catilina for this crime—(a sufficient proof of the degradation of public morals)—therefore the Roman criminal law could not take any cognisance of it, and it had to go unpunished.

15. quas omnes: "which in a complete form "; the English idiom would often put *omnes* with *ruinas* in the principal clause; the Latin order of words emphasises the adjective, as in *quae nullo debetur,* vii. 3.

16. proximis Idibus: the Kalends and Ides of the month (sometimes the Nones) were the usual days for payments of all kinds to be made. As Catilina's plot was now exposed and frustrated, his creditors would all be down on him at the next settling day.

18. difficultatem: " pecuniary embarrassments."

19. atque ad . . . vitam: *atque* or *ac* is often used to heighten the effect of what is coming, and introduce an idea that will come home to the audience or reader. Cp. in ii. 8, *mors ac rei publicae poena* and the note thereon. For *omnium nostrum* see note on *parens omnium nostrum* in vii. 24.

21. cum scias: " seeing that you know "—causal subjunctive.

22. pridie Kalendas Ianuarias: *i.e.* December 31st, 66 B.C. This refers to the first conspiracy; see Introduction, §§ 3 and 6.

23. in comitio: in the singular the word means the meeting-place of the *comitia, i.e.* the general assembly of the people for passing laws, electing magistrates, etc. A space at the N.W. of the Forum was appointed as the *comitium* of the *Comitia Tributa,* though they often met on the Campus Martius for elections, and elsewhere. As we have seen above, v. 15, the *Comitia Centuriata* met usually on the *Campus Martius.*

25. non mentem aliquam: Cicero says *mentem* to make a rhetorical antithesis to *furori* (sanity and insanity); but as *mentem* was after all not a good word to express what he really meant, *i.e.* a change of purpose or repentance, he adds *aliquam*, the force of which is to make the meaning of *mentem* wide and vague, or to apologise, as it were, for using the expression. This is often the force of the indefinites *aliquis* and *quidam*; cp. *quadam declinatione* below, l. 31, and *quodam modo* in vii. 28, on which see notes. If Cicero had meant " not any reflection " (= no reflection at all) he would have used *ullus* or *quisquam*.

27. neque enim . . . non multa: note that *neque* negatives both predicates, and *non multa* must be closely connected.

30. petitiones: " thrusts "; the terms here used seem to be technicalities borrowed from gladiatorial sword-play.

31. parva quadam . . . corpore: *quadam* softens down the boldness of the metaphor; *ut aiunt* does the same more emphatically. In *corpore* there is an implied antithesis to some such word as *armis*: the notion is that of a combatant who wards off blows by the agility of his movements, not by defensive armour. Cp. Vergil, *Aeneid*, V. 438 : *Corpore tela modo atque oculis vigilantibus exit,* " Only with his body and watchful eyes does he escape the blows."

33. tibi iam extorta est: some verbs signifying " to take away " have a dative of the indirect object, which may be classed as a dative of " advantage " or " disadvantage "; cp. vii. 38, *hunc mihi terrorem eripe,* " take this terror from me." Or *tibi* may be considered an ethic dative : " how often *have you seen* your dagger wrested from your hand ! "

35. quae quidem quibus: *quae* (= *et ea*) is the relative used, as often, as little more than a conjunction; *quibus* is interrogative, introducing the indirect question dependent on *nescio* : " to what sacred service."

abs te: this form of the preposition is hardly ever found except with *te*.

initiata sacris ac devota: assassins sometimes dedicated their weapon to a god, just as a victor would often give his weapons or some other trophy as a votive offering to a temple. But *sacris* may possibly be ablative of instrument: " with what sacred (or perhaps, accursed) rites "; popular rumour credited the conspirators with the drinking of human blood and other such ceremonies.

36. quod eam necesse putas: *quod putas,* not " because you think," but " in view of the fact that you think "; i.e. *quod putas* is a substantival phrase used as an accusative of reference. *Necesse* is the strongest word of its kind, and is used of a thing from which there is no escape, or to which one is bound down.

Ch. VII. 3. quae tibi nulla debetur: " which is in no wise your due," an emphatic form of negative; cp. note on vi. 15, *quas omnes senties.*

paulo ante: adverbs like *ante* and *post* contain a comparative notion; hence the word expressing *how long* before or after must take an ablative form, " before by a little," just as we say *decem annis ante* (" earlier by ten years "), or *maior dimidio* (" greater by half "). The ablative is that of measure.

5. **post hominum memoriam:** " within (lit. since) the memory of man," or as we might say " in all history." The word " history " is generally best translated by some phrase with *memoria*.

6. **contigit nemini:** the verb is generally used of fortunate occurrences, as *accido* is of misfortunes, while *evenio* is used indifferently of either; but there is no absolute rule in the matter.

vocis: genitive of material, like *taciturnitatis* in the following line.

8. **quod . . . vacuefacta sunt:** this clause, and the parallel one that follows (*quod . . . reliquerunt*), are substantival, and are taken up and summarised by *hoc*, which is the accusative (subject) with the infinitive *ferendum* (*esse*).

9. **qui tibi . . . constituti fuerunt:** a dative sometimes occurs that we find it convenient to call " dative of the agent," and to translate as though it were the ablative with *a* or *ab*. In reality it has the usual dative notion, expressing the person interested in or affected by the action of the verb. This dative of the agent occurs regularly with gerund and gerundive, and sometimes with perfect participles passive and the tenses formed with them, as well as with verbal adjectives in *-bilis*; otherwise very rarely. The text is better translated " who in your mind have been marked out for slaughter," than by saying " marked out by you." The form *constituti fuerunt* implies a past state (as opposed to *constituti sunt*, a past act or present state).

10. **nudam atque inanem reliquerunt:** an instance of the proleptic use of the adjective, expressing the result of the action of the verb.

11. **quo tandem animo:** *quo* is the interrogative, long deferred for rhetorical effect, which is heightened by the use of *tandem*, as at the beginning of the speech. Note that *quid* at the beginning of the sentence is not the usual interrogative, but means (as in iii. 21) " and then again."

13. **servi mehercule:** the latter word is a common exclamation, a corrupted and shortened form of some oath by Hercules, who seems to have been a popular hero in early Italian legend; though how far he can be identified with the Heracles of Greek story is uncertain. *Servi mei* is strongly emphasised by its position before *si*.

si me isto pacto metuerent . . . putarem: the conditional sentences in this section are instructive. The use of the imperfect (or pluperfect) subjunctive denotes that the case supposed does not (or did not) occur, and asserts its non-occurrence. Here Cicero, to strengthen his argument, is taking an extreme and practically impossible case: " If my very slaves feared me to such an extent—

which is not the case—I should have to run away from my own
home." Cp. note on *si te timerent*, l. 22 below. Contrast with these
forms the condition expressed by present subjunctives, which sometimes cannot, in the nature of things, occur, but the speaker assumes
its occurrence for the sake of argument; he takes " a hypothetical
case " as we often say. In, *e.g.*, Livy xxxix. 37, *si exsistat hodie ab
inferis Lycurgus*, " supposing Lycurgus were to rise up before us
from the dead," the thing is impossible, but the speaker does not
assert the impossibility, but disregards it for the sake of argument.
The student who carefully notes conditional forms will observe
that—

(i) The forms with the indicative imply (*a*) things that do or
may occur, and (*b*) a strict regard for the tense or time notion,
past, present, and future. In consequence of (*a*) *si* often means
" when " or " as," *e.g.* above, l. 5, *si hoc contigit nemini, vocis exspectas
contumeliam?* See also notes on *si aquam biberunt*, xii. 9; and on
convincam, si negas, iv. 6.

(ii) The past subjunctive forms assert the non-occurrence of the
condition, as we have seen above.

(iii) The present subjunctive forms denote a purely hypothetical
and unlimited supposition from which the distinctive notions of
(i) and (ii) are eliminated. Cp. note on *si tecum patria loquatur*,
viii. 1. The usual explanation that the present subjunctive forms
are used to denote a possible action in the immediate present or
future is misleading, as in normal instances both the time notion
and the question of possibility and impossibility disappear. And
as these forms approximate much more nearly in meaning to the past
subjunctives than to the indicative forms, the traditional classifica-
tion of future indicatives with present subjunctives is again somewhat
misleading.

15. tu tibi urbem: supply *relinquendam esse*; thus *tibi* is the
dative of the agent with a gerundive.

16. iniuria suspectum: " wrongfully suspected." The ablative
iniuria is practically an adverb, and so does not need *cum* or an
epithet, as the ordinary ablative of manner does. Cp. above, ii. 29,
iure and note.

22. si te . . . timerent . . . concederes: here again the past subjunctives denote what is contrary to fact; though in this case the
negative idea is prominent in the apodosis (principal sentence)
rather than in the protasis (or " if " clause). Cicero means " you
would depart (which you refuse to do now) if your parents feared
you."

24. nunc: " as it is "; *i.e.* to pass away from a supposition
contrary to fact to a real fact.

parens omnium nostrum: cp. this with *de nostro omnium
interitu* in iv. 11. As a rule the possessive adjective must be used,

and not the genitive of the personal pronoun, *e.g.* " my father " is *meus pater,* never *pater mei,* and Cicero observes this rule in cases where the possessive adjective comes before *omnium.* But where *omnium* precedes, he uses the genitive of the pronoun, *nostrum,* treating it apparently in this case as a possessive genitive. The irregularity is probably due to assimilation. *Nostrum* is, of course, usually a partitive genitive, but it is not so here, as " all of us " must be *nos omnes* and never *omnes nostrum.*

25. **nihil te . . . cogitare:** connect these words; *nihil* is emphasised by its position.

26. **parricidio suo:** Catilina's murderous schemes were directed against his *patria,* the *communis parens,* and are therefore called *parricidium. Suo* takes the place of an objective genitive.

28. **quodam modo:** " if I may so say "; to soften the boldness of the following expression.

tacita loquitur: an instance of " *oxўmōron* " (= pointedly foolish), an intentionally self-contradictory expression. Cp. Horace's *splendide mendax,* " nobly false "; and *cum tacent clamant,* viii. 32.

29. **aliquot annis:** the ablative expressing the " time within which " a thing is done.

31. **neces:** the plural is uncommon. The historical reference is to the proscriptions of Sulla.

sociorum: *i.e.* the provincials of Africa whom he misgoverned.

32. **quaestiones:** originally special commissions (*quaestiones extraordinariae*) to try cases that were too complicated to be dealt with by the assembled citizens, or *comitia.* The first of these was appointed in 413 B.C. Then *quaestiones perpetuae,* " standing commissions," were established—the first in 149 B.C.; and Sulla in his *régime* extended and organised them into a complete system of criminal courts, presided over by the praetors and additional presidents (*quaesitores*).

33. †**evertendas:** *v.l. evincendas,* a word often used of passing by a dangerous place in safety.

perfringendasque: as often, *que* is disjunctive, and to be translated " or."

36. **quidquid increpuerit:** lit. " whatsoever has sounded," *i.e.* " at every sound we hear." Note that the subjunctive is due to the oblique or reported form of the sentence: ordinarily *quisquis* and *quicumque* take the indicative.

37. **abhorreat:** this word in most cases has lost its original strong force, and means simply " to be disconnected," or " inconsistent with."

38. **hunc mihi timorem eripe:** the underlying metaphor is that of a nightmare or haunting incubus. As before noted, some verbs of " taking away " have the indirect object in the dative.

Ch. VIII. Consult the Index for Lepidus, Marcellus, Metellus, Sestius.

1. **si . . . patria loquatur . . . debeat:** Cicero above boldly and unconditionally represents the state as speaking. Now he puts it as a supposition, and adopting the conditional form with the present subjunctive, he says, " Supposing our country were to speak thus with you." He does not imply either that she does so speak or that she does not. See note on vii. 12.

2. **quid, quod . . . dedisti:** *quid* marks the transition to a new idea, when the latter is expressed by a rhetorical question. Here some verb must be understood, to which the substantival clause *quod . . . dedisti* will be the complement. The idiom is common, and identical in English and Latin. " Then again, what of the fact that you gave ? "

3. **in custodiam:** i.e. *libera custodia*, a sort of " house-arrest " in which a citizen might be placed pending his trial. He was not imprisoned, but (unless ordinary bail was taken) placed in the charge of some man of good position, who was responsible for his safe keeping. Catilina had been indicted under the *lex Plautia de vi* (*i.e.* for " inciting to riot ") by L. Aemilius Paullus, and had offered as a blind to submit to *custodia*.

4. **a quo:** equivalent to *et ab eo.*

8. **qui . . . essem:** the verb must be subjunctive as the sentence is in the indirect form; but the direct form, Cicero's actual words, might well have contained a causal subjunctive, *qui . . . sim*, " inasmuch as I am "; *qui* would thus be equivalent to *cum ego.*

10. **†M. Metellum:** nothing is known of this Metellus, if such is his name. *M. Marcellum* is found in some MSS.

11. **videlicet:** this marks the irony of the passage.

14. **a carcere atque a vinculis:** the general term for " imprisonment " or " prison " is *vincula*; the term *carcer* generally means the state prison or *Tullianum* at the foot of the Capitoline hill, which was not used for penal imprisonment, but for the safeguarding and execution of important criminals. Lentulus and other Catilinarian conspirators were strangled there. (*Carceres* generally means the barriers which formed the starting-point for races in the arena.)

qui . . . indicarit: the subjunctive may be explained in two ways. Either (1) the antecedent of *qui* is an implied *is*, and *is qui* = *talis ut is* = " a man such that he has judged ": in which case we have the consecutive subjunctive denoting a class (hence sometimes called the " generic " subjunctive). Or (2) the antecedent is " he," that is Catilina, contained in *videtur*; and *qui* = *cum is* = " inasmuch as he "; *i.e.* the subjunctive is " causal " or gives a reason for the main statement. In this case Cicero in speaking has turned from Catilina to the general audience.

17. in aliquas terras: " to some other part of the world." The plural *terras* must mean more than " country." *Aliquas* might also have the force of *nescio quas*, " some place or other, I do not care where."

19. refer . . . ad senatum: a technical term; the consul, or some other high official, who summoned the senate, would preside; and he alone could lay before them (*referre*) the matter to be discussed. He also collected their individual *sententiae* (*i.e.* opinions, with or without remarks), as we have seen above, iv. 13.

20. si . . . placere decreverit: the senatorial decree is reported as a statement (accusative and infinitive), not as a command (*ut* and the jussive subjunctive). Note that *obtemperaturum esse* (not *dicis*) is the apodosis to *decreverit*, which is subjunctive because the clause is a " reported condition." The direct form would be *si decreverit* (future-perfect indicative), *obtemperabo*.

21. non referam, id quod, etc.: *id* is in apposition to the idea contained in *referam* alone, not to *non referam.* Cicero seems to pose as a clement and not vindictive man; cp. ii. 15 and vii. 1-3. But his real reason was that the senate constitutionally had no power to act as a judicial court and sentence Catilina.

24. proficiscěre: after this word Cicero pauses to see if there is any expression of contrary opinion. As there is none, he continues and points the moral thereof to Catilina.

27. auctoritatem: in a concrete sense, " expressed authorisation."

30. fortissimo viro: this and such-like expressions are only complimentary commonplaces.

31. vim et manus: " violent hands "; hendiadys: cp. above, note on ii. 8.

33. cum tacent clamant: an oxymŏron, but more artistically introduced than before: see vii. 27, *tacita loquitur.*

34. auctoritas est videlicet cara: for *videlicet* marking irony see above, viii. 11, *quem tu videlicet*, etc. Cicero probably is thinking of Catilina's offer quoted in viii. 19.

35. illi equites: " the knights yonder "; cp. note on iv. 21.

36. ceterique . . . cives: the ordinary citizens who formed a third class after the senatorial and equestrian *ordines.*

37. tu . . . voces . . . exaudire potuisti: *tu* is strongly emphasised. Catilina could hear them, as well as see them, as he entered the senate; or perhaps the reference is to their applause in the course of the speech. The temple doors were open.

quorum . . . contineo: a concessive subjunctive *contineam* (" though I have long been keeping ") might be thought more natural here; but it would have partly spoilt the rhetorical effect Cicero gets from his elaborately balanced antithesis.

40. haec . . . relinquentem: *haec*—" all this "—would be accompanied by a gesture pointing to what was visible of Rome around them, and would suggest the Roman world generally.

41. ad portas prosequantur: *i.e.* they would escort him and " see him off," as friends, and no longer want to kill him.

Ch. IX. Consult the Index for Forum Aurelium, Manlius.

1. te ut ulla res frangat: like the exclamatory use of the accusative and infinitive, this exclamation must depend on some principal verb understood. It seems to be an indirect question form. *Ulla* is used because of the implied negative, " nothing will break you down."

4. duint: an archaic form of the subjunctive (for *dent*) used in prayers and adjurations; here it is jussive (or optative) subjunctive. The same formation with *i* is seen in *sim, velim,* etc.

video, si . . . induxeris, quanta . . . impendeat: the hypothesis is reported in the form of an indirect question depending on *video.* The direct form implied is *si induxeris* (future-perfect indicative), *quanta tempestas impendet,* where the apodosis would normally be a simple future; futurity, however, is implied in the meaning of the word *impendet;* " is threatening " = " will come."

7. sed est tanti: a genitive of value, " but it (*i.e.* the risk of unpopularity) is worth so much," *i.e.* the risk is worth running.

8. ista . . . calamitas: the word *calamitas* is mostly used of ruin in public life, seldom for " calamity " in the general sense. *Ista* = " that of yours," *i.e.* that you bring on me.

10. temporibus rei publicae: *tempora* = circumstances of the time, and so often " a political crisis."

11. is es . . . ut te . . . revocaverit: " you are not the man to have been recalled " (turn by the passive in English). An excellent instance of the consecutive subjunctive that we have generally noticed before after a relative. For *ut te* we should more often find *quem.* Distinguish carefully between (1) *is es qui hoc facias,* " you are the (kind of) man to do this," *i.e.* a general type; (2) and *is es qui hoc facis,* " you, who are doing this, are the man," where *facis* makes a definite statement about an individual.

15. praedicas: distinguish carefully *praedĭcāre,* " to declare openly," from *praedīcĕre,* " to predict."

conflare invidiam: a metaphor (from forge work) very common in Cicero. Note that *invideo* and *invidia* are much wider in meaning than the English " envy ": the notion in Latin is that of strong and general dislike, *i.e.* " odium " or " unpopularity."

rectā: understand *viă,* but still a distinctly adverbial phrase, " straightway."

18. sustinebo: *sustinēre* means to bear up against a weight or attack, and the metaphor is nearly always plain. *Sustentare* means to " sustain " (*i.e.* maintain or keep), apart from this notion.

19. importuna: the literal meaning of the adjective seems to be " out of place," but usually it takes its force from the context, and may mean anything bad.

21. latrocinio: " brigandage." *Latro* was a term originally applied to mercenaries, and often to irregular troops who would keep and pay themselves by marauding, like Turkish Bashi Bazouks. Cicero uses the term here to correct the previous *bellum*, which was too dignified a term to apply strictly to the Catilinarian revolt.

ut . . . videaris: here (as often) the notion of purpose (final subjunctive) blends imperceptibly with that notion of result (consecutive subjunctive) which denotes a natural consequence that may be expected and not a result that actually does happen. The negative *non* must be taken with *eiectus,* and does not affect the verb.

24. quamquam: " and yet." It should be noted that all the relative forms are constantly used, not as introducing a subordinate clause, as in English, but as mere co-ordinating conjunctions combining with another word. Thus *quamquam* is written rather than *et tamen*; and *cum* with the indicative is sometimes to be explained as being simply the equivalent of *et tum.*

invitem: deliberative (dubitative) subjunctive; " why should I invite ? "

a quo iam sciam esse praemissos: equivalent to *cum a te sciam,* " seeing that I know "; the subjunctive is thus causal. The subject of the infinitive is the implied antecedent of the *qui* following, *i.e. eos* or *homines* or some such word.

25. qui . . . praestolarentur: the prevailing notion in this subjunctive is that of purpose; *qui = ut ii.*

26. cui sciam . . . constitutam: the so-called " dative of the agent "; see on vii. 9, *tibi . . . constituti fuerunt*. But the dative here seems to stand in contrast with *a quo* that precedes and follows, and the distinction may be kept up in English: " when I know that a day has been settled to suit you."

27. aquilam illam argenteam: as before (vi. 35), Cicero charges Catilina with degrading superstition. Sallust tells us the eagle was a military standard that Gaius Marius had had when he defeated the Cimbrian hordes. Catilina posed as a popular leader, and so as a successor to the great democratic general Marius; and the standard was a sort of fetish to him.

28. perniciosam ac funestam: the Catilinarians thought it would bring them luck.

29. sacrarium scelerum: *sacrarium* was firstly " a chapel " or " shrine " as a repository for any sacred objects; then the religious idea faded out, and the word was used for any secret repository. Thus the meaning here is " for which the secret chamber of your crimes was made into a holy shrine." A further underlying notion in the words is suggested by the fact that in the Roman camp the spot by the *praetorium* (headquarters) where the eagles were kept was regarded as sacred.

30. tu ut illa . . . possis: the exclamatory form noticed on ix. 1.

32. altaribus: this word is only used in the plural in good Latin.

Ch. X. 1. ibis tandem aliquando: Cicero here takes up the thread of argument interrupted by § 24. The word *aliquando* simply gives rhetorical emphasis to *tandem*. The thought is, " Go forth to Manlius; and then you will at last reach the goal you have long been speeding towards."

quo te iam pridem . . . rapiebat: the imperfect denoting the beginning of an action, " began long ago to whirl you." Usually the imperfect with *iam pridem* denotes that the action had been going on for some time (" had long been whirling you ").

3. haec res: *i.e.* not merely beginning civil war (as some explain), but, more generally, Catilina's joining Manlius and all that that involved; partnership in foul debauchery as well as *nefarium bellum*.

4. voluntas: by this word Cicero often means " political inclinations " or policy, and probably does so here.

5. non modo otium . . . concupisti: *non modo = non modo non ;* for the first clause, *non modo otium*, must be completed by supplying from the next clause the necessary words, including the negative from *ne . . . quidem*. Thus we get *non modo non otium nisi nefarium concupisti*, " you not only did not want peace, except a wicked one, but you did not even want," etc. Cp. this with *non modo se non contaminarunt, sed etiam honestarunt*, in xii. 7 below. In this latter case *non modo non* must be written in full, as the first sentence is complete in itself; moreover the second has no negative that could be supplied even if wanted. It must also be noticed that the negatives in the two clauses of the text do not cancel the negative in *numquam*, but simply repeat it. This is common when a sentence, starting with a negation, is continued in two branches, as Cicero, *Ad Atticum*, 14, 20, *Nemo umquam neque poeta neque orator fuit*. . . .

8. conflatam: " welded together," a common metaphor in Cicero.

9. laetitia perfruēre . . . gaudiis exsultabis: *laetitia* is a stronger expression than *gaudium*; hence the latter has the more expressive verb, *exsultare*, lit. to " leap " or " dance," hence to " run riot " in delights.

10. bacchabere: " revel " like a mad or drunken votary of Bacchus.

11. virum bonum quemquam: *ullum* would be commoner, as *quisquam* is generally substantival.

12. meditati: " practised." The perfect participles of many deponents sometimes bear a passive sense: e.g. *comitatus, veneratus*.

illi . . . qui feruntur labores: *labores* = bodily exertions for physical
"training." Sallust describes Catilina as a man of great bodily
endurance. *Qui feruntur*, "which are so generally talked about."
Or possibly we should treat *labores* as a predicate with the copulative
verb *feruntur*, and regard *illi* as agreeing with *labores* by assimilation: "those (practices) which are called 'training,'" *i.e.* "that
'training' as it is called."

13. **iacere humi**: this, as well as *vigilare* below, is in apposition to
labores. The phrases suggest the hardships of a soldier's or hunter's
life; but there is a coarse *double entente* throughout. Note that
humi is an instance of the locative case, like *domi, ruri*, etc.

14. **ad facinus obeundum**: "for the prompt performance of
crime "; *obire* (= to go to meet) sometimes acquires the meaning of
promptly attending to matters of business. Cp. Cicero, *De Amicitia*,
§ 7, *diligentissime semper illum diem et illud munus solitus esses obire*,
" you were always wont to be punctual to the day and its duties."

15. **insidiantem**: in agreement with the accusative *(te)* implied
as subject of the infinitive *vigilare*.

16. **otiosorum**: men peacefully sleeping with no idea or fear of
any attack on their property.
habes, ubi ostentes: "you have (an opportunity) where you may
show "; *ubi = ut ibi*, so that in it; the subjunctive is consecutive.

17. **patientiam famis**: objective genitive.

18. **quibus**: agreeing with the antecedents *famis, frigoris, inopiae*.

19. **tantum profeci**: "this much at any rate I accomplished," *i.e.*
I did not crush the outbreak, but I kept such a foul creature as I
have described out of office. This is possibly an answer to criticisms
made on Cicero's action at the election: see next note.

a consulatu reppuli: this must refer, not to Cicero's successful
candidature against Catilina in 64 B.C., but to the election of consuls
for the year 62, over which Cicero, as consul in 63, would preside:
see v. 15, *seq.* Cicero had appeared on the Campus Martius with a
strong armed guard and overawed the armed adherents of Catilina,
who meant to carry his election by force. The use of the indicative
with *cum* shows that the subordinate clause is represented as merely
marking the time of the principal clause.

exsul . . . consul: an intentional paronomasia or word-play.

21. **†quod esset**: the mood is subjunctive because the clause is
dependent on another subjunctive (*ut . . . nominaretur*). Others
read *est*, which would imply that the relative clause was not part
and parcel of the consecutive clause, but a sort of explanatory note
interjected, like *quo debeo* in vii. 2.

22. **bellum**: Catilina had been pronounced *hostis patriae*; and
had he been armed with consular *imperium* he might have been
described as making *bellum*.

Ch. XI. 1. **quandam** has an apologetic force: " if I may so say."

2. **detester ac deprecer:** " turn from myself by prayer (*i.e.* to the gods) and entreaty (*i.e.* to you)."

3. **quae dicam:** a relative and future indicative, not a dependent question with the subjunctive.

5. **si . . . loquatur:** " suppose my country were to say "; for the form of the conditional sentence see notes above on vii. 12 and viii. 1. Owing to the length of the following appeal, the sentence is left without an apodosis.

10. **non emissus . . . sed immissus:** another word-play; *emissus* suggests a discharged prisoner or defaulter, *immissus* a weapon hurled.

ut . . . videatur: a subjunctive exactly parallel to *ut videaris* in ix. 20 above, where see note.

12. **duci . . . imperabis:** Cicero and Caesar sometimes use a passive or deponent infinitive with *impero* instead of *ut* with the subjunctive. Distinguish *dūci* from *dŭci* (*dux*).

16. **an leges:** the second part of a compound question, hence *an.* Supply the verb *impediunt* from *impedit* above. The earliest of these laws was the *Lex Valeria* (509 B.C.), which secured the right of appeal (*provocatio*) to the people against a magistrate's sentence of scourging or death. The principle was reasserted and strengthened by the *Lex Porcia* (197 B.C.), and by the *Lex Sempronia* (121 B.C.) of Gaius Gracchus. Jurisdiction concerning the *caput* of a Roman citizen was in Cicero's time delegated to *quaestiones*, which could not inflict the death penalty. See Introduction, § 5.

17. **rogatae:** any proposition was put to the *comitia* in the form of a question: " Is it your sovereign will and pleasure ? " Hence *rogare legem*, " to bring forward a law," a phrase here loosely used for to pass it.

18. **invidiam posteritatis:** subjective genitive; contrast with the genitive *severitatis invidia* below, l. 24.

20. **refers gratiam:** " repay a debt of gratitude." Distinguish *gratiam habere*, " to be grateful," and *gratias habere* or *agere*, " to give thanks."

nulla commendatione maiorum: none of Cicero's ancestors had held a curule office; hence he was styled a *novus homo*, not a *nobilis*.

21. **tam mature:** the earliest age at which a Roman citizen could be a candidate for the various *honores* or high offices of state was fixed by the *Lex Villia Annalis* (180 B.C.). Cicero elsewhere boasts that he alone of *novi homines* attained the consulship in the earliest possible year. He was now forty-three.

22. **per omnes honorum gradus:** according to the *leges annales* of Sulla the *gradus* or order in which the offices were to be taken was

as follows: quaestorship, praetorship, consulship. The aedileship, though not legally necessary, was generally held after the quaestorship, on account of the opportunity it afforded of conciliating the voters by magnificent shows and games.

24. si quis . . . metus: the form *quis* is used both substantivally and adjectivally; but *qui* (nominative singular masculine) is adjectival only.

26. cum . . . vastabitur: " while Italy is being devastated "; not the usual future-perfect, because the action is coincident in time with that of the apodosis verb, *conflagraturum.* Notice the correspondence of the two verbs. The latter is put into the infinitive by *existimas*; and strictly speaking the subordinate verbs *vastabitur,* etc., should have been in the subjunctive as indirect or reported forms. But Cicero began the sentence with the intention of finishing with *tu non conflagrabis?* and then, with a change of thought, slightly altered the form of his apodosis.

28. conflagraturum: the metaphor from fire is very common in Latin and Greek. The verb *flagrare* is constantly used of a man whose reputation is blasted.

Ch. XII. Consult the Index for Flaccus, Gracchi, Saturninus.

2. sentiunt: the word is often used of political opinion: cp. *cum Caesare sentire,* " to belong to Caesar's party "; and xiii. 19, *quid de re publica sentiat.*

3. si . . . iudicarem: " if I thought " (which I do not), or " if I had thought " (which I did not: continuous past action). Contrast *dedissem,* " I should have given " (simple past act).

4. usuram: in its literal sense of " use " or " enjoyment."

gladiatori: slaves, trained to arms, often accompanied the leaders of faction at this time in Rome, when street brawls were frequent, such as the fray between Milo and Clodius. Hence *gladiator* = hired assassin or cut-throat.

5. summi viri: such as those mentioned before in Ch. II.

6. Flacci: called Fulvius before in ii. 5.

9. quid . . . invidiae: join these words, the latter being a partitive genitive.

parricida civium: the murderer of a citizen was a *parricida,* partly because it was a sin against the *patria,* the *communis parens;* and partly because it was the murder of a brother, and the term *parricidium* applied to the killing of any near relation.

10. si . . . impendēret . . . fui: an irregular but common form of sentence; in which the speaker begins with a hypothesis, then, suddenly changing the form of sentence, continues with an unconditional assertion of fact followed up by something equivalent to an apodosis. " Even if odium had been threatening me—well, my idea

always was," etc. The correct apodosis to *si . . . impenderet* would
have been some such sentence as *invidia, virtute parta (ut opinor)
gloria esset, non invidia;* but the intruding idea *hoc animo fui* ousts
the real apodosis from its natural position as principal sentence and
makes it a consecutive clause. This chiefly occurs when the apodosis
becomes an accusative and infinitive; cp. note on xi. 25. Distinguish
impendĕret from *impendēret.*

13. **quamquam**: " and yet."

in hoc ordine: *i.e. ordine senatorio.*

qui . . . ea quae imminent non videant: note carefully the
moods here and in the following clause. *Qui non videant* denotes a
class (whom the *imperiti* will follow), " such fools that they do not
see "; hence the subjunctive is consecutive, in the form sometimes
called the " generic " subjunctive. But we have the indicative in
quae imminent (although it is subordinated to a subjunctive clause)
because Cicero wishes to represent the threatened perils as distinct
and individual facts. So *dissimulent* marks the class from whom the
improbi will take their cue.

14. **dissimulent**: *simulo* is to invent something non-existent;
dissimulo to hide what exists.

15. **mollibus**: *mollis* is perhaps a contraction of *mobilis,* and means
" easily moving," and so fickle or shifty; then in a secondary sense
" yielding," and so soft or effeminate.

aluerunt: the indicative because it is virtually the principal
verb of a new sentence; *qui . . . aluerunt = et hi . . . aluerunt.*

17. **multi**: *i.e.* many outside the senatorial order.

19. **regie**: " despotically "; an invidious meaning clung to the
word *rex* and its congeners, perhaps from the memory of the Tarquins.

20. **pervenerit**: the apodosis verb is *fore,* put into the infinitive by
intellego.

21. **qui non videat**: as before pointed out, Cicero uses this form
much more often than *quin.*

22. **hoc . . . uno interfecto**: the ablative absolute is equivalent to
a protasis *si hic interfectus sit* (representing the future-perfect
indicative, which would have been used if the sentence had not
been subordinated to *intellego*); the apodosis verb is *reprimi posse.*
In the latter it should be noted that, instead of the normal future,
the modal auxiliary (*possum*) with its infinitive is used; and thus
the awkward substitutes (*fore ut,* or the supine with *iri*) for the
wanting future infinitive passive are avoided. The difficulty of
the future subjunctive passive can often be met in the same way,
by using *possum* or some other auxiliary of mood.

Ch. XIII. 2. **nescio quo pacto**: *nescio quo* is regarded (and may
be written) as one word, an indefinite pronoun; consequently it does
not affect the mood of the verb *erupit.* The whole phrase expresses

(euphemistically) a feeling of discontent; "heaven only knows why."

4. **tanto latrocinio**: the abstract for the concrete, "such a horde of brigands": cp. *coniuratio* for conspirators (iii. 3).

6. **cura et metu**: ablatives of separation.

8. **aestu febrique**: practically hendiadys, "fever heat."

9. **iactantur**: *cum* with the indicative here denotes frequentative (or iterative) action; and the following *si biberunt* is equivalent to *cum biberunt*, "whenever they drink." Cp. note on *cum*, iii. 15.

11. **relevatus**: equivalent to a protasis, *si relevatus erit*.

12. **reliquis vivis**: ablative absolute.

16. **tribunal praetoris urbani**: there were eight praetors at this time, with functions chiefly judicial. Six took charge of the criminal courts, while the *praetor urbanus* and *praetor peregrinus* heard civil suits, the latter taking those in which a foreigner was concerned. The *praetor urbanus* had a permanent tribunal in the Forum, and an attempt had been made to intimidate him in the decision of certain debt cases.

cum gladiis: "sword in hand," a rather common phrase, which must never be confused with the ordinary instrumental ablative without a preposition.

17. **curiam**: *i.e.* the *curia Hostilia*, the original senate-house, said to have been built by the king Tullus Hostilius, on the north-east side of the Forum. It was burnt down in the riots following the death of Clodius, 52 B.C. The senate could meet only in a *templum, i.e.* a spot definitely marked out and duly consecrated.

malleolos: a mallet-shaped missile with a wire head filled with some inflammable material, and having a barbed point to enable it to fasten on to woodwork, etc.

18. **sit denique inscriptum . . . sentiat**: if the Catilinarians all left the city and joined the rebels at Faesulae, they would be coming out in their true colours and confessing their political views. By *inscriptum in fronte* Cicero probably intends to suggest a comparison with slaves who were branded on the forehead for various offences.

25. **hisce ominibus**: the "omens" were the prophecy contained in the words he had just used.

28. **tu, Iuppiter, qui . . . constitutus**: Cicero here turns to the statue of the god in the temple. His language is somewhat exaggerated, as the temple was not built under Romulus, who, according to the legend, vowed it; it was only much later, in 294 B.C., that the senate ordered its erection.

SECOND SPEECH.

Ch. I. 1. tandem aliquando: emphatic, " at length and at last."

Quirites: the Roman citizens in their civic capacity. This oration was delivered at a *contio* or meeting of the Roman people convened by a magistrate (in this case by Cicero as consul) in the Forum. Cicero in order to make an impression on his motley audience indulges freely in rhetorical artifices and extravagant expressions which would be quite out of place in the Senate.

3. ferro flammaque: ablatives of instrument.

4. vel . . . vel . . . vel: *vel* is an imperative form from *volo*, and means " take your choice." It is used where the choice is a matter of indifference or concerns the expression only. Cicero is afraid that he will offend the populace if he uses only the more forcible term, *eiecimus*.

ipsum: " of his own accord."

5. abiit: this and the three following words form a kind of climax.

6. monstro . . . atque prodigio: hendiadys, " pestilent portent."

moenibus: dative of disadvantage.

7. atque . . . quidem: " yes indeed."

9. sica illa: " that dagger of his."

10. campo: sc. *Martio*. The Campus Martius was a plain in Rome formed by a bend in the Tiber : here the *comitia* met, and the Romans took their exercise.

foro: the Forum, or market-place, was an open space between the Capitol and the Palatine. It was used for judicial business as well as for commercial purposes.

curia: the Curia Hostilia, or senate-house, stood at the northwest corner of the Forum.

11. loco: ablative of separation. The metaphor is from boxing; " post of vantage."

12. cum . . . depulsus: the indicative with *cum* here denotes identity of action; *cum* = " in that." So also below, *cum . . . coniecimus*.

17. vivis nobis: ablative absolute.

ei: dative of indirect object after a verb of taking away.

20. iacet: " he is on the ground."

22. profecto: " we may be sure."

23. quae quidem: " which for its part."

24. evomuerit . . . proiecerit: subjunctives of reported cause; the reason for the exultation of the city is represented as one assigned by the city itself.

Ch. II. 1. oportebat: *i.e.* when Catilina might have been seized. Impersonal verbs like *oportet* in a historic tense are followed by the present infinitive, where in English the perfect infinitive is used.

3. accuset: consecutive subjunctive.

capitalem: " deadly."

4. comprehenderim . . . emiserim: these verbs are in the subjunctive, as the cause is represented as alleged at the time of action.

7. mos maiorum: " tradition."

huius imperii: the reference is to the dictatorial power conferred by the senate on the consuls in grave crises; the senate then passed the decree called *senatus consultum ultimum*, by which the ordinary laws were suspended and the consuls were directed to provide " that the state suffer no harm " (*ne quid respublica detrimenti capiat*). This power had been conferred on Cicero and his colleague on October 22nd, the day after that on which Cicero had publicly attacked Catilina in the Senate. For the illegality of the decree see Introduction, § 5.

9. deferrem: subjunctive by assimilation with *crederent.*

crederent: consecutive subjunctive. The words in square brackets are a gloss.

14. invidiae . . . vitae: genitives in dependence on *periculo.*

meae: = *mei*, objective genitive.

15. vobis: dative of person judging.

16. morte: ablative denoting the penalty.

multassem: representing future-perfect indicative of direct speech.

17. rem huc deduxi: " I brought the matter to this point."

19. videretis: subjunctive in dependence on the final subjunctive *possetis.*

20. putem: subjunctive in indirect question, depending on *intellegatis.*

21. intellegatis: jussive subjunctive in semi-dependence on *licet.*

22. comitatus: the perfect participle of a deponent verb is rarely (as here) passive in meaning.

exierit: subjunctive of reported cause.

23. eduxisset: the pluperfect subjunctive with *utinam* expresses a wish with regard to the past.

mihi: ethic dative, " to my relief."

24. in praetexta: sc. *toga*, " in boyhood "; boys under sixteen wore a toga bordered with a band of purple (*praetexta*).

26. poterat: historic tenses of *possum* are constructed with the present infinitive where English idiom requires the perfect infinitive.

aere: ablative of description.

Ch. III. Consult the Index for Gallicus Ager, Apulia, Gallia, Metellus, Picenum.

1. Gallicanis legionibus: the troops stationed in winter quarters in Cisalpine Gaul (for which see Index, *s.v.* Gallia).

4. collectum: referring to *exercitum*.

5. agresti luxuria: abstract for concrete = *agrestibus luxuriosis,* " country profligates."

decoctoribus: " bankrupts "; *decoctor* is from *decoquo,* " to boil down," and so " to run through " (one's property).

6. vadimonia deserere: " to run away from legal obligations." These persons left their homes for Catilina's army without putting their affairs in order; since they left no legal representatives behind them, a declaration of bankruptcy (*missio in possessionem*) would follow, and their property would be seized and sold.

exercitum: sc. *deserere.*

7. quibus ego . . . si: = *qui, si ego iis.*

8. edictum praetoris: the praetors (who had control of civil jurisdiction at Rome) on their entrance to office announced by means of edicts (decrees or proclamations) what their rulings in law would be in any given case. The edict " contained rules which were the extension of legal principles to new classes of facts," and aided, supplemented, or corrected the civil law. Here that part of the edict which dealt with *vadimonia* (see line 6) is referred to.

11. purpura: the purple stripe on the edge of the *tunica laticlavia* (" broad-striped tunic ") which was worn by senators and military tribunes of the equestrian order.

mallem: potential subjunctive; the imperfect is used of something that may not be realised.

suos milites: " as his personal retinue."

eduxisset: jussive subjunctive in semi-dependence on *mallem.*

13. nobis: dative " of agent " (really a dative of the indirect object) with *pertimescendos.*

14. hoc: causal ablative = " on this account."

quid cogitent: object of *scire.*

quid cogitent me scire: object of *sentiunt.*

15. cui sit Apulia . . . Gallicum: for Apulia, etc., see Index. C. Manlius (see Index) had been sent to Faesulae in Etruria, Septimius Camers to Picenum, C. Julius to Apulia.

17. sibi: " for his share," with *depoposcerit.*

insidias: " secret schemes."

18. caedis . . . incendiorum: genitives of definition, or that in which a thing consists.

superioris noctis: " the night before last "; the reference is to the meeting of the conspirators in the house of M. Porcius Laeca which took place on the night of the 6th of November; the first speech against Catilina was delivered on November 8th, and the present speech on November 9th; Cicero is therefore hardly exact in his statement.

20. **hesterno die:** *i.e.* in the first speech against Catilina, November 8th.

21. **ne:** " certainly "; this word is sometimes written *nae*; it has no connection with *ne,* " lest."

Ch. IV. Consult the Index for Aurelia Via.

2. **aperte:** with *videretis.*

3. **videretis:** subjunctive in consecutive clause.

nisi vero si = nisi vero: " unless indeed "; *nisi* has full adverbial force in this phrase.

Catilinae: objective genitive with *similes.*

cum Catilina sentire: " to hold the same views as Catilina."

6. **exeant, proficiscantur:** jussive subjunctives.

ne patiantur: *patiantur* is probably subjunctive in final clause, " that they may not suffer," *not* jussive subjunctive.

sui: objective genitive with *desiderio.*

7. **Aurelia via:** see Index.

9. **O fortunatam rem publicam:** the accusative in exclamations is really the object of some verb vaguely understood.

sentinam: " bilge-water," hence " refuse."

10. **uno Catilina exhausto:** the metaphor in *sentina* is kept up.

11. **mali . . . sceleris:** partitive genitives.

12. **conceperit:** consecutive subjunctive.

13. **tota Italia:** the ablative of " place where " is used without a preposition in the case of nouns qualified by *totus* or *medius.*

14. **testamentorum subiector:** " forger of wills "; *subicio* means " to substitute " false for true; hence " to forge."

15. **circumscriptor:** a cheater or despoiler of wards or minors; cf. Juvenal XV., v. 135, *pupillum ad iura vocantem circumscriptorem.*

19. **nefarium stuprum:** " abominable debauchery."

per illum: " through his means " (*not* " by him ").

21. **iuventutis:** objective genitive with *inlecebra,* " genius for enticing youth."

24. **impellendo . . . adiuvando:** the ablatives of the gerund are here equivalent to present participles: " while at the same time instigating," etc.

27. **non modo Romae, sed ne ullo quidem in angulo,** etc.: the regular expression is *non modo non,* etc., but *non modo* is used for *non modo non* when the predicate (here *fuit*) is common to both clauses. Translate, " not only at Rome, but even in any corner," etc. The original negative *nemo* is not destroyed, but merely repeated by the *non* understood after *modo,* and by *ne . . . quidem.* We may also consider the regular *non* after *modo* to be contained in *nemo* (= *non*

. . . *quisquam*); "not only not at Rome, but not even in any corner . . . was there anyone," etc.

30. **sceleris**: either (1) objective genitive or genitive of the remoter object, almost equivalent to *ad scelus*; or (2) genitive of description or material, "criminal conspiracy."

Ch. V. 1. **in dissimili ratione**: "in matters of a different kind," "in a different sphere (lit. 'method') of life," *i.e.* from that just dealt with.

diversa studia: ("diversity of tastes or pursuits") refers to his association at one time with gladiators, at another with stage-players.

2. **ludo gladiatorio**: a "school" where slaves were trained to be gladiators under a *lanista* or fencing-master.

3. **audacior**: *i.e.* than the rest.

4. **in scaena**: "on the stage." Actors were as a rule slaves or freedmen; if a Roman citizen became an actor he was considered to be degraded (*infamis*).

5. **sodalem**: member of the same political guild or coterie (*sodalitas*). Such clubs managed canvassing by means of election agents, and the members were bound to support one another.

6. **stuprorum**: objective genitive.

7. **frigore, etc.**: *assuefactus* can be used either with the dative or (as here) with the ablative (of instrument).

8. **cum**: "although"; the clause is concessive.

industriae . . . virtutis: objective genitives. The reference is to the resources or powers which in Catilina's case were put to an improper use.

10. **sui**: we might have expected *eius*, since the reference is not to the subject of the sentence; but *sui* here = "his own proper."

14. **humanae**: natural to mankind, and therefore such as one may excuse.

16. **fortunas**: "estates," "landed property."

obligaverunt: "encumbered" by mortgage.

res . . . fides: "money . . . credit." Their creditors had begun to lose confidence in them, owing to the failure of the plot.

19. **comissationes**: "revels" followed by torchlight processions and music.

21. **possit**: potential subjunctive.

25. **obliti**: from *oblino*, "smear," not from *obliviscor*, "forget," which would require *obliti*.

31. **nescio quod**: with *breve tempus*, "for some short time."

32. **propagarit**: *propagare* is properly a technical term in gardening, meaning "to grow by means of layers"; suckers which are allowed

to grow from the parent stem and take root before being severed are called *propagines*. Here the word is used metaphorically to mean "extend," and so "secure," with object denoting the time which is secured (for the State).

33. pertimescamus: subjunctive in consecutive relative clause.

34. unius: the reference is to Pompeius, who was engaged in the settlement of the East, after his destruction of the pirates (*mari*) in 67 B.C. and his defeat of Mithradates (*terra*) in 66 B.C. He made the Euphrates the frontier of the empire, covered it by new provinces, and secured it by client-states. See also Pompeius in Index.

40. quacumque ratione: sc. *potero*: "as best I may."

42. et in urbe et in eadem mente permanent: by the figure called syllepsis, *permanent* is used in the first clause in a literal, in the second clause in a metaphorical, sense: cp. Vergil, *Aeneid II.*, v. 654. "*inceptoque et sedibus haeret in isdem.*"

Ch. VI. Consult the Index for Faesulae, Iuppiter Stator, Laeca, Manlius, Massilia.

1. a me . . . exsilium: the emphasis is on these words. So far from having been driven by Cicero into exile, Catilina had departed of his own free will to join his followers in their camp at Faesulae.

2. verbo: "by a single word."

4. videlicet: ironical; the word = *videre licet*, "anyone can see." permodestus: *modestia* is the virtue of one who is easily amenable to discipline, or has proper respect for duly constituted authority.

6. hesterno die: on the 8th of November. See Introduction, §§ 3, 6.

8. patres conscriptos: see note on I., Ch. II. 15 (p. 76).

12. principes: those who had held the office of consul (*consulares*).

14. hic: the narrative is here resumed after the parenthesis *quo cum . . . reliquerunt.*

15. nocturno conventu: this meeting was most probably held on the night of November 6th. See Introduction, §§ 3, 6.

16. necne: when the latter alternative is contradictory of the former, *necne* is used in indirect, *annon* in direct, double questions.

17. conscientia: sc. *culpae:* "consciousness of guilt."

19. ei: dative of agent.
ratio: "plan" of campaign.

20. teneretur: reflexive, "involved himself."

21. pararet: subjunctive in dependence on the dependent subjunctive *dubitaret.*

22. secures . . . fasces: these were tokens of *imperium* ("right to command"). No one except a magistrate entitled to *fasces* could take the field at the head of Roman citizens. Catilina, though he

had been defeated in his candidature for the consulship, sought to give a show of constitutional authority to his position as a revolutionist by assuming the insignia of a consul.

23. **aquilam illam argenteam:** see note on I., Ch. IX. 25.

24. **sacrarium:** a place in which a sacred object (*sacrum*) is kept, a "shrine." The spot in a Roman camp near the *praetorium* ("general's tent") in which the eagles were kept was looked upon as sacred.

fecerat: the indicative is here used as the relative clause is introduced by Cicero for the information of his hearers, and not as part of the words addressed to Catilina.

25. **eiciebam:** imperfect expressing attempted action.

27. **populo Romano:** dative of disadvantage with *indixit*.

suo nomine: " on *his own* account "; *suo* is emphatic.

29. **Massiliam:** see Index. Catilina gave out that he had retired to Massilia in order that peace might be preserved.

30. **haec castra:** the same as **illa castra** above; *haec* is used in contrast with the more remote Massilia.

Ch. VII.   Consult the Index for Manlius, Massilia.

1. **condicionem:** " terms," hence " arrangement," " task."

5. **ex:** " (turning aside) from," " instead of."

7. **armis:** ablative of separation with *spoliatus*.

audaciae: genitive of material, or that in which a thing consists; it is here equivalent to *audaciā*, in apposition with *armis*: " that weapon of his—his audacity."

10. **vi et minis:** hendiadys, " violent threats."

13. **velint:** consecutive subjunctive.

est mihi tanti: the subject of *est* is *huius . . . subire*.

tanti: genitive of value, a variety of the genitive of quality.

22. **illud:** the pronoun refers to what follows; it can generally be rendered by " this."

23. **emiserim . . . eiecerim:** subjunctives reporting the cause assigned for Cicero's unpopularity; " because (as people will say) I have induced him to go," etc.

24. **profectus sit:** subjunctive in concessive clause; *cum* = " though."

26. **Catilinam Massiliam ire:** " that Catilina is on his way to Massilia."

27. **nemo,** etc.: Catilina's professed friends pretend to pity him because he has been forced into exile; but this pity is not sincere, it is only feigned. If it were really genuine, they would prefer that he should be safe at Massilia rather than in the utmost danger of defeat and death at the camp of Manlius.

29. **ille autem,** etc.: Catilina would in any case rather die in arms than live as an exile. But since his present course is the result, not of impulse, but of intention, we ought to pray that he may go into exile rather than complain at the idea of his doing so.

Ch. VIII. 1. et . . . non timeo: after *et* supply *quem* from *qui*.

3. **interest:** *i.e.* between him and me.

4. **dissimulant:** sc. *se esse hostes,* " who dissemble their enmity." *simulo* means to pretend that a thing exists when it does not; *dissimulo* means to pretend that a thing does not exist when it really does exist.

6. **sanare sibi ipsos, placare reipublicae:** " to restore (lit. ' heal ') them to their (true) selves, to reconcile them to the State." The adherents of Catilina are represented as no longer under control of their highest or rational selves. For *sibi ipsos* we might expect *sibi ipsis,* but the pronoun generally agrees with the subject or object of the verbs, not with the reflexive pronoun.

9. **generibus hominum:** " classes of society."

10. **singulis:** sc. *generibus.*

consilii . . . orationis: either subjective genitives, or genitives of that in which a thing consists. *medicina* generally takes an objective genitive denoting that to which the remedy is applied.

11. **quam:** sc. *medicinam adferre.*

eorum: genitive of definition, or that in which a thing consists: " one class consists of those . . . "

13. **maiores . . . possessiones:** their estates would, if sold, be more than sufficient to pay their debts.

14. **dissolvi:** the passive is here used as a direct reflexive, one of the uses of the middle voice in Greek : " to disencumber themselves " (*i.e.* of debt and of their estates).

16. **causa:** " case," " position."

impudentissima: because they might have defrayed their debts by selling their property; this want of principle showed that they were impervious to a sense of shame.

tu, etc.: Cicero rhetorically addresses one of the class he is characterising.

argento: " silver-plate "; this was often elaborately chased.

17. **ornatus et copiosus:** a kind of hendiadys; " abundantly supplied."

sis: deliberative subjunctive, an interrogative form of the jussive subjunctive: " are you to," etc.

20. **sacrosanctas:** rendered " inviolable " by a religious act, so that anyone injuring them would become *sacer,* accursed.

21. **tabulas novas:** " fresh accounts," a common expression for the cancelling of debts; by the destruction of old account-books and the

substitution of new ones debts were sometimes abolished as one result of a successful revolution. Catilina had promised his partisans that he would cancel all debts.

22. **meo:** in contrast with *Catilina*.

auctionariae: sc. *tabulae*. These were catalogues of the goods to be sold by auction. As *tabulae* (properly " writing-tablets ") would be used both for the entering of debts and the list of goods to be sold, Cicero is enabled to indulge in a play of words which can hardly be preserved in English. Perhaps " accounts " here and in the preceding line would represent the general sense. Cicero here refers to his intention of introducing a law by which debtors would be forced to sell their estates by auction and pay their debts with the proceeds. Thus the auctioneers' *tabulae* would be *novae*, since they would be the result of a new law, and would lead to the cancelling of debts, the common meaning of *tabulae novae*.

24. **salvi:** " safe " from bankruptcy, *i.e.* " solvent."

25. **certare cum usuris fructibus praediorum:** lit. " to contend against the interest (on their debts) with the proceeds of their estates," *i.e.* to strive to pay the interest out of the income derived from the estates. Since the interest was always the larger sum of the two, the contest was a hopeless one for the debtors.

fructibus: instrumental ablative.

26. **locupletioribus . . . melioribus civibus:** predicative.
uteremur: " we should find."

Ch. IX. Consult Index for Manlius, Sulla.

2. **dominationem:** " absolute power."

3. **honores:** " offices."

6. **ut . . . posse:** a final clause giving the *purpose* of the warning; the actual warning is contained in the accusative and infinitive clauses, *primum omnium . . . laturos.*

12. **vim sceleris:** " criminal violence "; *sceleris* is genitive of definition or material.

praesentes: " mighty to aid," hence " propitious "; often used of deities in this sense.

13. **sint . . . adepti:** subjunctive denoting a remote or improbable contingency; in the apodosis the indicative *sperant* and the accusative and infinitive is substituted for the regular subjunctive; contrast *adepti sint . . . sit* below.

17. **quod:** object of *adepti sunt* and subject of *concedi*; *quod concedi* is subject of *necesse sit*; *sit* is regular present subjunctive in apodosis of a conditional clause containing a future condition regarded as remote and improbable.

20. **exercitatione:** ablative of means.

21. **ex iis coloniis quas Sulla constituit:** for Sulla see Index. In

82–81 B.C. Sulla confiscated the lands of the revolted communities, and on the *ager publicus* thus acquired he settled 120,000 of his veterans; he thus sought to provide for the re-population of Italy, to form a kind of reserve army for the senate, and to restore small holdings (now practically extinct) and with them the agriculture of Italy. Most of these military settlements were in Etruria.

22. **civium . . . virorum:** predicative genitives.

23. **sed tamen ii sunt coloni:** " but still those men (*i.e.* those who form my third class) are colonists who," etc., *not* " there are some settlers who," since *qui* is here followed by the indicative, not by the consecutive subjunctive.

in: " in the midst of."

26. **beati:** " men of wealth."

familiis: " establishments of slaves."

28. **velint:** subjunctive in a clause dependent on *sit*, which is subjunctive in a dependent (consecutive) clause.

29. **atque:** " aye and," " and even "; *ac* and *atque* lay emphasis on the second of the two words connected by them.

30. **veterum:** " of former days," = *antiquarum*. For the reference see note on line 33 below.

quos utrosque: *i.e.* the *coloni* and the *agrestes*.

31. **praedatorum:** genitive of definition, or that in which a thing consists.

eos: referring to the whole class, *coloni* and *agrestes* alike.

32. **proscriptiones . . . dictaturas:** like those of Sulla (see Index). Proscriptions were published lists of persons who could be put to death with impunity. The Sullan proscriptions included 4,700 names.

33. **illorum temporum:** *i.e.* the time of the Marian massacre (87 B.C.) and of the Sullan proscriptions. For Marius see Index.

34. **non modo homines sed ne . . . pecudes quidem:** as the predicate (*passuri esse videantur*) of the second clause is already negatived by *ne quidem*, and is also the predicate of the first clause, a second *non* after *non modo* is not expressed, but must be understood. Translate " not only men, but even brute beasts, do not seem," etc.

Ch. X. 1. **turbulentum:** " heterogeneous."

5. **vadimoniis, iudiciis, proscriptione bonorum:** the three stages in the procedure against a bankrupt: (1) both parties made an appointment (*vadimonium*) binding themselves in a sum of money (*satisdatio*) to appear in court on a certain day; (2) the case was sent by the praetor before a *iudex*, and the actual trial (*iudicium*) took place; *iudicium* here also includes the judge's decision (*sententia*); (3) in case the defendant (*i.e.* the debtor) lost and did not pay his debts within 30 days, the plaintiff could seize his goods,

publish a list of them to be sold by public auction, and finally have them sold for his own benefit. *Proscriptio bonorum* is properly the list of the goods to be sold, but here it also includes the sale itself; translate " public sales by auction of their property."

7. **infitiatores:** *infitiator* is properly one who " denies " or shirks payment of a debt; there is also here a side allusion to the shirking of military service.

9. **corruant:** jussive subjunctive.

non modo, etc.: see note on Ch. IX., l. 34.

13. **pereant:** subjunctive in a comparative conditional clause, putting an imaginary case; the apodosis is not expressed.

16. **pereant:** jussive subjunctive.

17. **carcer:** the state prison (and only prison) in Rome was situated under the Capitol; it was only used for the execution of prisoners, or as a place of detention during trial.

19. **genere:** " character."

20. **de eius dilectu:** " his chosen friends," lit. " (friends) from his selection."

21. **nitidos:** " spruce," " spick and span."

imberbes: a sign of effeminacy.

bene barbatos: " with full-grown beards," a sign of foppery; as a rule no Roman grew a beard unless he were in mourning for some one.

22. **manicatis:** " with long sleeves " reaching to the hand.

talaribus: " reaching to the ankles " (*tali*). It was a sign of effeminacy to wear tunics that reached below the knee.

velis amictos: people fond of display wore broad togas, which swept the ground; this was an offence against propriety.

23. **vitae . . . vigilandi:** genitives of the remoter object, equivalent to prepositional phrases.

27. **neque:** sc. *solum.*

spargere: " to sprinkle," *i.e.* " to mix " (in drinks).

29. **hoc:** for *hos* by attraction into the gender and number of the secondary predicate *seminarium,* " a nursery."

31. **num:** expects the answer " no ": " surely they don't intend to take," etc.

33. **Appenninum:** the Apennines, the mountain chain which is the backbone of Italy.

Ch. XI.   2. **scortorum:** genitive of material or definition.

cohortem praetoriam: " body-guard "; a guard of 500 friends to protect the person of the general was first organised by Scipio Aemilianus at the siege of Numantia (133 B.C.).

6. **eiectam:** " cast on shore," " stranded."

8. **urbes:** here " walled towns."

coloniarum ac municipiorum: partitive genitive: " such of the towns of the colonies and municipia as are walled." Colonies were originally either Roman or Latin; and only the Roman colonies had full citizenship. Municipia were originally states whose citizens had the private but not the public rights of Roman citizens. As a result of the Social War (91–88 B.C.) all the Italian states obtained the full Roman franchise, and the *coloniae* and *municipia* became country towns of Roman citizens.

respondebunt: " will answer for themselves to," *i.e.* " will be a match for."

12. **quibus:** ablative of instrument with *suppeditamur,* and of respect with *eget.*

13. **vectigalibus:** properly the due paid by the occupants or lessees for their tenure of parts of the domain-land in Italy. The word *vectigal* was also applied to the rent or due (in money or produce) paid by owners of land in the provinces; for provincial land was held to be *ager publicus* of the Roman people. Indirect taxes such as port-dues and frontier-dues were also called *pecuniae vectigales.*

15. **causas:** " principles."

16. **velimus:** subjunctive in protasis of conditional clause expressing a vague future condition; in the apodosis one would expect a corresponding subjunctive; but the potential idea is contained in *intellegere possumus,* which is practically equivalent to *intelligamus.*

19. **pietas:** sc. *erga patriam,* "loyalty "; *pietas* is a general word meaning " dutiful conduct "; its meaning is specialised according to the context.

20. **honestas:** " honour "; this word never means " honesty."

24. **ratio:** here of *political* " principles."

27. **deficiant:** the present subjunctive in the apodosis denotes the *improbability* of human enthusiasm failing.

Ch. XII. Consult the Index for Gallicus Ager, Metellus, Picenum.

3. **mihi:** dative of agent, not uncommon with the perfect participle passive.

tumultu: " alarm of war."

4. **coloni omnes municipesque vestri:** " your fellow-citizens in all the colonies and municipia "; see note on Ch. XI., l. 8.

9. **tamen:** this word refers to *quam . . . putavit,* not to the *quamquam* clause, which is parenthetical.

15. **atque adeo:** " or rather."

19. **adhuc:** with *lenitas:* " my clemency up to this point."
solutior: " somewhat remiss."

23. **portis:** dative, not ablative; lit. " for the gates."

25. **cuius:** = *si illius.*

28. **carcerem:** *i.e.* as a place of execution, not of imprisonment as a punishment.

30. **voluerunt:** " decreed," " ordained."

Ch. XIII. 3. post hominum memoriam: " within the memory of man."

4. **togato:** dressed in the *toga*, the garb of a civil magistrate, instead of the *paludamentum*, the cloak of a military magistrate.

9. **illud:** refers to *ut . . . possitis.*

10. **vix optandum:** " almost beyond the reach of prayer," " almost past praying for."

11. **neque bonus . . . paucorumque:** rare for *neque . . . et.*

poena: ablative of price: " at the cost of the punishment of a few."

14. **deorum:** subjective genitive.

15. **significationibus:** " intimations," " prodigies."

quibus: the antecedent is *deorum*, not *significationibus.*

17. **ab externo hoste et longinquo:** with *defendent.*

20. **quam urbem . . . hanc:** = *hanc urbem quam; urbem* is attracted into the relative clause.

THIRD SPEECH.

Title. oratio tertia habita ad populum: *orationem habere* is " to deliver a speech "; *orationem facere* is " to compose a speech."

Ch. I. 1. rem publicam: this and the following accusatives form the object of the verb *videtis*, l. 7.

Quirites: this was the title by which the citizens were addressed in their civil capacity as Roman burgesses. The term is probably derived from an old word *quiris*, meaning " a spear," so that the original sense was " spearmen." Another derivation was current among the ancients, from the Sabine town, Cures.

vestrum: this is the partitive gentive of *vos*, the objective genitive being *vestri.*

bona: " your property "; in this sense the word is used only in the plural, *bona, bonorum, n.*

2. **atque:** this word carries on the summation to something higher still. The threatened burning of their city was the item in Catilina's programme which more than anything else raised the fury of the people.

4. hodierno die: equivalent in meaning to the adverb *hodie*. The Senate had on that day (December 3rd) passed a resolution, by which four of the leading conspirators (Lentulus, Cethegus, Statilius, and Gabinius) were placed under immediate arrest, upon their crime being brought home to them by the evidence of Volturcius and the Allobroges; and an order had been at the same time issued for the arrest of five more.

6. fati: " of destruction "; cp. *exitii ac fati diem*, vii. 24.

ereptam, conservatam, restitutam: these words agree grammatically with *urbem*, but in sense with the other accusatives also, *rem publicam*, etc.

7. si non minus iucundi sunt: the apodosis (result clause) is *esse in honore debebit is qui . . . ;* in conditional sentences of this type not so much a condition is implied as an *a fortiori* argument supplied from fact. Instead of using the conditional form it would be possible to express the same thing by *ut . . . ita*.

8. illustres: the word here bears its primary meaning of " clear," " bright."

quibus: abl. of time when.

9. nascendi incerta condicio: " the issues of our birth uncertain "; *i.e.* the circumstances into which we are born. No one knows whether his life is destined to be one of wretchedness or of happiness.

10. cum voluptate: ablative of manner with the preposition *cum:* the phrase is in strict contrast to *sine sensu.*

11. profecto: an adverb compounded of *pro* and *facto*, and meaning " assuredly."

illum: *i.e.* Romulus.

12. ad deos immortales: Romulus after death was worshipped as a deity under the title of Quirinus, and his festival, the Quirinalia, was celebrated on the 17th February in each year.

benevolentia famaque sustulimus: " in gratitude and renown we have raised "; this deification is the work of men and is the outward expression of the kindly feeling (*benevolentia*) and the words of adoration (*fama*) with which we perpetuate the memory of our founder.

13. esse . . . debebit is: " that man will be bound to be held."

15. toti urbi: this is the dative of the indirect object after *subiectos* and *circumdatos.*

templis delubris: *templum* is a space consecrated by the augurs, and may even refer to a portion of the heavens; *delubrum* is a place hallowed by the presence of a deity. In ordinary language the words are frequently combined, in which case *delubra* may be taken as equivalent to " shrines," conveying an idea of deeper sanctity than *templa.*

16. idem: " we too "; nominative plura masculine, agreeing with *nos* understood.

17. destrictos: *destringere* means " to unsheath," " draw from the scabbard." *Retundere,* which usually bears the secondary meaning " to blunt," must here be translated " to beat back," " strike down."

19. quae quoniam: the relative followed by a conjunction is best translated by " and " with the demonstrative, " and seeing that these things." Note that *quoniam* is followed by its regular mood, the indicative.

20. per me: " through my instrumentality "; the position is emphatic.

21. quanta: nominative plural neuter subject of *sint.*

qua ratione: " in what manner "; the expression is equivalent in meaning to *quo modo.*

22. sint: the subjunctive mood is necessary here, because the clause is an indirect question depending upon *scire.* The direct question would be, *Quanta et . . . comprehensa sunt?*

et exspectatis: " and eagerly await information."

possitis: this is the present subjunctive after *ut,* denoting purpose and following the primary tense *exponam.*

23. principio: an adverb (originally an ablative of time when), " first of all." Cicero is anxious to explain at the outset that there has been no lack of energy on his part, and that the delay in taking active measures against the conspirators has arisen from the difficulty of obtaining palpable proofs of complicity.

ut: *ut* followed by the indicative means " as " or " when "; rarely, " since."

paucis ante diebus: " a few days ago ": the ablative is one of measure, and *ante* is an adverb (lit. " before by a few days "). Cicero makes little of the interval of time which had elapsed since Catilina's flight. This speech was delivered on the evening of December 3rd, and Catilina had quitted the city in the early morning of November 9th.

erupit: " he burst out "; this is the word used by Cicero in his Second Oration (Ch. I.) as a climax—*abiit, excessit, evasit, erupit.*

24. huiusce: a strengthened form of *huius,* consisting of the genitive and the enclitic *-ce.*

25. Romae: "at Rome"; this is the locative, a case which in singular substantives of the first and second declensions is identical with the genitive.

reliquisset: the subjunctive mood must follow *cum,* when the time is past, unless absolutely nothing but the time of the action is indicated, so that the *cum*-clause marks the date merely, without any other relation such as concession or cause. In the passage before us, " cause " is implied, " seeing that he had left."

27. possemus: subjunctive, because the clause in which this verb occurs is a dependent question, introduced by *quem ad modum* (how) and dependent upon the perfect tense *providi.*

Ch. II. Consult the Index for Allobrŏges, Flaccus, Gallia, Lentulus, Pomptinus, Reāte, Volturcius.

1. **eiciebam:** the indicative mood here follows *cum,* because time alone is indicated, " at the time when I was endeavouring to drive out "; contrast *cum . . . reliquisset,* i, 25. Cicero by openly denouncing Catilina as an enemy of the State had all along intended to drive him out of the city—the climax of his denunciations was reached, when he delivered his speech in the Senate on November 8th, known as the First Catilinarian Oration, which had the desired effect—for, that very night, Catilina departed. *Eicere* is a strong word, which Cicero used with hesitation and as an alternative expression in the Second Oration (Ch. I.); but which now, after the production of palpable proof of Catilina's villainy, he no longer fears to employ.

non . . . iam: " no longer."

2. **illa:** sc. *invidia,* " odium." The precise cause of odium is explained by the clause *quod vivus exierit.*

sit: the subjunctive mood follows *cum,* both for present and past time, when it means " since," " inasmuch as."

3. **exierit:** this is the perfect subjunctive, which mood is necessary because *quod* does not refer to Catilina's departure as a fact, but as the ground of the *invidia,* " because, *as people complain,* he got out of the city alive."

exterminari: this verb (from *ex* and *terminus,* " boundary ") means " to expel," " exile."

5. **restitissent:** pluperfect subjunctive of *resto;* the subjunctive mood is used in clauses dependent upon an accusative and infinitive mood—subject to the general exception, that the indicative mood is required in a clause which indicates a permanent independent attribute of a specified person or thing. Cp. *sciebam,* ii. 7.

6. **atque ego:** " and so I "; the meaning of this passage is— " accordingly, finding that I had been mistaken, I did my best to unearth all their plottings in the city, and so effectually and palpably to bring their guilty designs to the light, that you might be roused to a sense of your danger, when it was thus presented to your eyes."

vidi: the indicative mood is used, because *ut* here means " when."

7. **eos:** as this word refers to particular persons, the verb in the relative clause *(sciebam)* is put in the indicative mood.

8. **in eo . . . ut . . . sentirem:** " in ascertaining "; lit. " in the endeavour that I might ascertain." The *ut*-clause is here explanatory of *eo.*

9. **quid agerent:** " what it was they were doing "; an indirect question depending upon *sentirem.*

ut: " in order that "; to be taken with *comprehenderem.*

10. **auribus vestris:** " in your ears "; a dative of advantage.

11. minorem: " too little "; lit. " less than it deserved."

fidem faceret: " was gaining credence "; the subjunctive mood is here used after *quoniam*, because the verb of the clause on which it depends (*comprehenderem*) is subjunctive. Instances of such assimilated subjunctives are common.

12. demum: the adverb serves to emphasise *tum*, " then at least."

animis: " with your minds," *i.e.* " heartily "; ablative of the instrument, in verbal antithesis to *oculis*.

15. tumultus Gallici excitandi: this is an example of gerundive attraction, in which the gerundive in agreement with the noun takes the place of the gerund with its object in the accusative. When the verb is one that governs the accusative case, this gerundive attraction is by far the more common construction. *Tumultus* always has reference to a disturbance in Italy or Gallia Cisalpina. *Causā*, like *gratiā*, " for the sake of," is regularly followed by a genitive.

a P. Lentulo: see Index, *s.v.* Lentulus.

16. eodemque itinere: " on the same route "; the homeward route of the Gauls would lie through Etruria, in the north of which Catilina was then encamped near Faesulae.

17. litteris mandatisque: " with written and verbal instructions."

18. ad Catilinam datas litteras: " letters for Catilina "; in the phrase *dare alicui litteras ad aliquem*, the dative refers to the messenger who carried the letter, often a slave specially kept for the purpose, and termed *tabellarius*.

19. ut . . . deprehenderetur: this clause cannot be said to be explanatory of *facultatem*; but, since this word is equivalent to *efficiendi occasionem*, we may understand the clause as consecutive to *efficiendi*, implied in *facultatem*. Some editors repeat the *ut*, placing a second *ut* before *tota res*, and explain the repetition as necessary, in order to pick up the sense after the interruption caused by the parenthesis *quod . . . immortalibus*.

23. hesterno die: equivalent to *heri*, just as *hodierno die* (i. 4) is to *hodie*.

24. praetores: the number of praetors at this time was eight, and their chief duty was to preside over the courts of law in the capital. When their year of office had expired they were sent to govern provinces.

rei publicae: genitive case dependent upon *amantissimos*; when a present participle is used simply as an adjective, it admits of degrees of comparison and may govern an objective genitive case.

25. vocavi: " I summoned "; the consuls, praetors, and of course dictators, possessed the *ius vocationis*, the right of summoning any citizen to their presence; cp. iii. 7.

26. qui . . . sentirent: the relative pronoun here does not merely intimate a fact, but indicates a cause; hence the subjunctive mood is used.

was too strong for him, and stoned them to death in the place where he had put them for safety.

42. **quo minus . . . occideret:** " so as to prevent him slaying." *Quo minus* and the subjunctive may be used after any expression denoting prevention.

de quo nihil nominatim erat decretum: " in whose case no decree had been issued "; as had been the case with Lentulus. But, as no decree of the Senate could override the laws, this is a mere oratorical flourish on the part of Cicero.

43. **praetorem:** the emphatic position of this word is to be noted, which brings out the antithesis between it and *privato*.

privato: " a private citizen," which Lentulus became after his resignation.

Ch. VII. 5. **pellebam:** the indicative may be used when *cum* means " at the time when," especially if its purely temporal character is emphasised by *tum* in the principal sentence.

6. **remoto Catilina:** ablative absolute expressing a condition, " if Catilina was removed."

mihi: dative of agent with the gerundive, *pertimescendam*, which refers to three substantives, but agrees with the last only.

Lentuli somnum: " the sleepiness of Lentulus "; see note on iii. 8.

9. **sed tam diu dum:** " but even he, only so long as."

10. **omnium aditus tenebat:** " he knew the weak side of every-body "; lit. " he held the approaches to all men."

11. **consilium:** " ability to plan ": the meaning of the sentence is—" he had natural skill in planning evil."

13. **certas:** " particular."

15. **quod non ipse obiret:** " which he did not himself take in hand "; the consecutive subjunctive is used here, because *quod* is equivalent to *tale ut id*.

16. **occurreret, vigilaret, laboraret:** these verbs are neuter, and the government of *quod* belongs strictly to *obiret* only.

20. **in castrense latrocinium:** " to his robber camp "; lit. " to the life of a bandit in his camp." Of course, the camp is that of Manlius at Faesulae.

23. **Saturnalia:** Lentulus had arranged that there should be a rising in Rome on the Saturnalia (December 19th). Cicero says Catilina would not have waited all that time.

24. **tanto ante:** " so long before the time "; *ante* is an adverb. The Saturnalia were still more than a fortnight distant.

25. **commisisset ut:** " committed the blunder of allowing," lit. " committed the mistake so that."

30. quodsi: " whereas if." In this word *quod* was originally an accusative of extent, " as to which thing."

31. fuit: the subject to be understood is *Catilina,* " as long as Catilina was here."

32. ut levissime dicam: " to treat the matter very lightly," " to say the very least."

dimicandum nobis fuisset: lit. " there would have been a conflict for us," *i.e.* " we should have had to fight it out."

Ch. VIII. 1. quamquam: adverb, " and yet." Cicero, having finished his account of the proceedings in the Senate, now alludes to the evidence furnished throughout of divine interposition.

3. cum . . . tum vero: " not only . . . but."

coniectura: " by inference "; we can infer divine interposition from the fact that the control of such vast movements was beyond human counsel.

4. quod: " because," " inasmuch as."

humani consilii: genitive of the predicate with *esse,* " to belong to the sphere of human wisdom," " to be within the scope of human counsel."

5. praesentes: " directly," " in very person."

7. ut omittam: final subjunctive; so *relinquam* and *omittam* below. *Illa* refers to what follows, *i.e.* the meteors and the blaze in the sky.

8. ab occidente: " in the west "; the preposition denotes locality not motion, as also in *a tergo,* " in the rear," *a latere,* " on the flank."

9. terrae motus: the usual expression for " earthquake."

10. nobis consulibus: " in our consulship," ablative absolute; of course this is the present year.

11. canere: " to foretell "; since the responses of oracles were delivered in verse, the verb *canere* came to have simply the meaning of " predict."

14. Cotta et Torquato consulibus: *i.e.* two years ago, namely 65 B.C.

15. de caelo esse percussas: *i.e.* the objects were struck by lightning, another expression for which is *de caelo tangi* (l. 17).

16. depulsa: " cast down " from the blocks of marble on which they stood.

17. legum aera liquefacta: by *legum aera* we are to understand bronze tablets or pillars, on which laws were engraved; fragments of some such tablets are still extant.

18. ille . . . Romulus: " the renowned Romulus "; the reference is possibly to the statue representing the wolf suckling the infants Romulus and Remus, which is still to be seen at Rome not far from its old site.

inauratum: " gilded "; the statue was of bronze.

19. **uberibus**: dative of indirect object after *inhiantem*.

22. **civile ac domesticum**: *ac* introduces a more emphatic adjective, " civil war, ay, a war against our hearths and homes "; cp. *atque* in *urbis atque imperii* in the same line.

25. **flexissent**: the pluperfect subjunctive here in *oratio obliqua* represents the future perfect in *oratio recta*. The future perfect would naturally be used in the subordinate clause, because *appropinquat*, the principal verb, is future in sense. The actual words would run: *urbis occasus appropinquat* (i.e. *urbs peritura est*), *nisi di fata flexerint.*

fata ipsa: " destiny itself." This illustrates the belief of the ancients that behind the gods there was the mysterious power of Fate, which even they were unable to resist.

26. **responsis**: " on their prophetic announcements "; ablative of cause. *Responsum* is strictly the reply of an oracle.

ludi: such celebrations ordained on special occasions by the Senate were called *imperativi*. The occasion might be either joyous or sad. In the latter case the days were spent largely in religious exercises.

27. **pertineret**: the subjunctive is employed here because *quae* is equivalent to *talis ut ea.*

28. **simulacrum Iovis**: the statue of Iupiter Optimus Maximus, which stood on a lofty pedestal in front of the Capitolium and was visible from the Alban Mount, a distance of fourteen miles.

29. **facere**: the subject of this infinitive can easily be supplied from the context.

in excelso: the neuter singular of adjectives of three terminations is often used substantivally with a preposition; cp. *de improviso,* " unexpectedly," *ex adverso,* " from the opposite quarter."

contra atque antea fuerat: " opposite to its former position." The use of *atque* with *alius* is similar; *e.g. alius sum atque tu* (lit. " I am different and you are different "), " I am different from you."

30. **ad orientem**: "towards the east"; so as to overlook the Forum.

31. **forum**: the *forum Romanum* was a long open space extending in a south-easterly direction from the base of the Capitoline Hill and lying between the Quirinal and Palatine Hills. It was surrounded by porticos (*basilicae*) and shops, and was the general place of meeting of the people. Towards its northern end was the *Rostra*, the platform from which the people were addressed; between the *rostra* and the Capitoline lay the *comitium*, the place in which the *comitia tributa* were held; and facing these, at the foot of the Capitoline, stood the Curia Hostilia, in which as a rule the meetings of the Senate took place. During the Catilinarian alarm the Senate met in the adjoining temple of Concord and in that of Iupiter Stator.

32. fore ut ea . . . illustrarentur: the common periphrasis, employed to avoid the use of the future infinitive (in this case, *illustratum iri*); lit. " that it would happen that these plots might be brought to light."

essent initia: *ineo*, " I enter upon," " form (a plot)," is transitive, and hence can be used personally in the passive.

34. illud signum collocandum . . . locaverunt: " put out to contract the erection of that statue "; with *locare*, " to put out anything to contract," and *conducere*, " to contract to do anything," the gerundive in agreement with the object expresses the work to be done; *e.g. secanda marmora locare*, " to put out a contract for having marbles quarried." This construction also occurs with *curare*, *suscipere*, and other verbs.

36. superioribus consulibus: *i.e.* the consuls of 65 B.C. and 64 B.C. This may be regarded as an ablative absolute, *superioribus* being equivalent to *superioribus consulibus*, " the consuls of the last two years being in office." With *nobis* is understood *consulibus*, " with me as consul," " in my consulship."

Ch. IX. 1. **hic:** adverb, " under these circumstances."

2. mente captus: " insane "; lit. " impaired in mind," *mente* being the ablative of respect; cp. the phrase *oculis et auribus captus*, " blinded and deafened."

qui neget: " as to deny "; the subjunctive is consecutive, *qui* being equivalent to *ut is*.

6. et ea: " and that, too "; with *ea* (neuter plural accusative) supply *comparari* as verb.

quae: the antecedent is *ea*, in the next line.

8. verum etiam: identical in meaning with *sed etiam*.

9. ita praesens: " so immediately the act of the gods in our midst." Just as the gods are described as *ita praesentes* (viii. 5), their action is here termed *ita praesens*. The clause *ut . . . videatur* is consecutive, " so that it seems."

10. ut, cum . . . statueretur: the whole of this clause is explanatory of *illud*.

11. meo iussu: " by my orders." *Iussu* is the only case in use of a defective noun of the fourth declension.

12. in aedem Concordiae: where the meeting of the Senate was being held. See note on viii. 30.

16. quo: ablative of cause, " on which account."

19. si . . . dicam, . . . sumam: the present subjunctive, in both protasis and apodosis, implies that the condition refers to future time and is still possible.

20. nimium: this is the neuter of the adjective used as a substantive.

ille, ille: here Cicero points to the newly-erected statue.

21. haec templa: there were several temples in the immediate neighbourhood of the Forum; the word *templa* is often used by Cicero to embrace the *rostra*, which had been consecrated. Neither the Senate nor the assembly of the Centuries could meet in any spot which had not been inaugurated with the due formalities.

22. dis . . . ducibus: ablative absolute, " with the immortal gods for my leaders."

23. hanc mentem: " this resolution, purpose."

24. iam vero: " further "; marking the transition to another point—the folly of the conspirators, which must have been sent by the gods, according to the saying *quem deus perdere vult, prius dementat.*

26. creditae: join with *essent.*

27. huic tantae audaciae: " from this outrageous audacity "; the dative is often found instead of the ablative and a preposition with verbs compounded of *ab*, *de*, and *ex.*

28. consilium: " wisdom."

quid vero ? *i.e. quid vero dicam?* the phrase marks another transition—to the god-inspired loyalty of the Gauls to the Roman state.

ut . . . neglegerent . . . anteponerent: explanatory of *id*, l. 33.

29. male pacata: " only partially reduced to peace." It will be remembered that Caesar only began his victorious career in Gaul five years later; at this date Roman authority was confined to the Provincia (later known as Gallia Narbonensis).

30. quae . . . videatur: *quae* is equivalent to *talis ut ea.*

34. praesertim qui: " especially seeing that they."

non pugnando, sed tacendo: the gerunds are here used as ablatives of manner.

Ch. X. Consult the Index for Catulus, Cinna, Lepidus, Marius, Octavius Sulla, Sulpicius.

1. pulvinaria: " couches "; see note on *supplicatio*, vi. 29.

7. togati: " in the garb of peace," *i.e.* to adopt modern phraseology, " as civilians "; the *toga* was the characteristic dress of a Roman citizen in contradistinction to the *sagum* of the soldier. Hence *togatus* often means " in the garb of peace "; the word is also used to denote Roman as distinguished from foreign. Cp. vi. 32.

9. vosmet: the particle -*met* may be added, by way of emphasis, to any case of the personal pronouns, except the nominative *tu*. It may also be added to certain cases of the adjective pronouns.

10. P. Sulpicium: for the proper names occurring in this section, the Index should be consulted: the references are all to events which had occurred little more than twenty years before, and so

were within the memory of many of the audience. The dates are as follows:—

88. P. Sulpicius Rufus proposes that the command in the war against Mithradates should be taken away from Sulla and given to Marius. L. Sulla marches with his army from Nola upon Rome, and compels C. Marius and Sulpicius to flee. Sulpicius is taken, but Marius escapes to Africa.

87. The consul Cn. Octavius, a partisan of Sulla, fights a pitched battle in the Forum against his colleague, L. Cornelius Cinna. Cinna is driven from Rome, but is joined by Marius, and the two combine to take Rome. In the massacres that follow Cn. Octavius, L. Caesar, and Q. Lutatius Catulus, the victor of Vercellae, perish.

83. Sulla returns from the East to avenge the death of his partisans.

82. By the battle of the Colline Gate Sulla becomes master of Rome. Five thousand citizens are proscribed, and many cities in Etruria and Samnium punished by wholesale confiscation of their lands.

77. M. Aemilius Lepidus tries to overthrow the constitution of Sulla, but is defeated in a battle fought in the Campus Martius by Q. Lutatius Catulus, son of the conqueror of Vercellae.

11. oppressit: "crushed"; cp. *interfectos aut oppressos*, xii. 4. custodem: after his defeat of the Teutones at Aquae Sextiae (102 B.C.) and of the Cimbri at Vercellae (101 B.C.), Marius was hailed as the saviour of the state.

12. partim: . . . partim: "in some cases . . . in others."

13. collegam: "his colleague in the consulship"; *i.e.* Cinna.

omnis hic locus: the conflict between Octavius and Cinna took place in the Forum.

14. redundavit: this word is joined to both *acervis* and *sanguine*, although strictly it is suitable only to the latter. This figure of speech is known as Zeugma ("a yoking"). Cp. in English, "See Pan with flocks, with fruits Pomona *crowned*."

20. ipsius: *i.e.* Lepidus. He could not have been popular with either party in the state, for the democratic faction could have had little confidence in a man who had enriched himself with the spoils of the Sullan proscriptions, while the *optimates* would despise him as an insincere renegade.

21. ceterorum: the genitive depends on *interitum*, and refers to the followers of Lepidus, who were involved in his fall.

23. quae: the relative pronoun is here consecutive, being equivalent to *ut eae*; cp. the construction following *eius modi*, below, line 28, and xi., line 7.

24. **rem publicam:** " constitution."

26. **conflagrare:** " to be burnt "; an intransitive verb.

28. **non reconciliatione concordiae:** " not by the re-establishment of harmony," implying that the result was not obtained without recourse to arms.

29. **diiudicatae sint:** according to the general rule of the sequence of tenses, this word should be *diiudicarentur*; but the perfect subjunctive is often found in a consecutive clause following a historic tense, when a specified result is indicated as having occurred on a specified occasion, so that the attention is to be directed rather to the result than to the conditions leading up to that result.

30. **uno . . . maximo:** " decidedly the greatest "; *unus* is sometimes added to a superlative to intensify its force.

post hominum memoriam: " since the memory of man," *i.e.* going back to the most remote period to which human knowledge extends.

32. **barbaria:** equivalent to *barbari*, " inhabitants of a barbarian land "; no civil war, Cicero says, even among barbarians, was ever so cruel as this, which has for its object the destruction of the capital city and the indiscriminate slaughter of fellow-citizens.

lex haec: " this principle "; explained by the following *ut*-clause, *ut omnes . . . ducerentur.*

a Lentulo, Catilina, Cethego, Cassio: when several proper names are connected in sense, it is usual either to place the conjunctions between each, or to omit them altogether.

34. **salva urbe:** ablative of attendant circumstance.

ducerentur: " should be reckoned."

36. **tantum:** " just so much "; the neuter singular is used as a noun and governs a partitive genitive. So *tantum urbis* below.

37. **restitisset:** " remained over from "; from *reso.* The pluperfect subjunctive represents here in *oratio obliqua* the future perfect indicative of direct speech. The words reported were—*tantum civium supererit quantum caedi restiterit.*

38. **obire:** *obeo* is here used in the sense " to reach," and *flamma* is the nominative.

Ch. XI. 2. **nullum . . . monumentum laudis:** " no memorial raised to my praise "; this is the objective genitive, as is the genitive in *praemium virtutis*, " reward due to merit "; *insigne honoris*, " mark of honour," such as an honourable title conferred upon one.

3. **praeterquam:** " except "; this word must be followed by the same case as is required by the verb, whereas *praeter* is used as a preposition governing the accusative.

5. **ornamenta honoris:** " honourable distinctions," *i.e.* honours of state.

6. mutum: " without the power of speech."

7. eius modi quod: " of such a kind that . . . it "; *quod* being the same as *ut id.* Cp. the example of similar construction in x. 22.

9. alentur . . . crescent . . . inveterascent: " shall be nurtured, shall grow up and be confirmed "; the different stages of growth are indicated by these words. *Res* may here be translated " exploits."

sermonibus: " the conversation of men."

litterarum monumentis: " the records of literature "—especially written history.

10. diem: " length of time." In the sense of " appointed day " *dies* is often feminine, and almost always so in the sense of " period of time." In the plural it is always masculine.

11. propagatam esse: " has been extended."

13. duos cives: *i.e.* himself and Pompeius. The latter had just completed his victorious campaign in the East, in which he had overthrown Mithradates of Pontus and received the submission of the latter's son-in-law Tigranes of Armenia.

exstitisse: the infinitive is dependent upon *intellego.*

15. terminaret: the subjunctive here follows *quorum,* which is equivalent to *tales ut eorum.* Note that after the perfect infinitive the dependent subjunctive is generally in the imperfect or pluperfect tense.

Ch. XII. 2. quae illorum: " as of those men ": the antithesis is not here logically maintained, persons (*illorum*) being contrasted with things (*earum rerum*).

5. ceteris facta sua recte prosunt: *se* and *suus* generally refer to the subject of the sentence, but may refer to some other word, provided that no ambiguity arises thereby. In this sentence *sua* refers to *ceteris.* For this use of *si,* see note on i. 7.

6. ne quando: " lest at any time "; after *si, nisi, ne, num,* instead of *aliquis* and its derivatives, *quis* and its derivatives are used. For his present action, Cicero was driven into exile five years afterwards.

7. ne vobis nocere possent ego providi: the leading clause is *ego providi,* the tense of the verb being perfect (not aorist) : yet the tense of the dependent subjunctive (*possent*) is imperfect. This modification of the general rule of the Sequence of Tenses is very usual after the perfect tense, unless the action in the dependent clause is strictly confined to present time. In the example before us, Cicero had not taken precautions against the citizens being harmed at that present moment, but all along.

9. mihi quidem ipsi nihil ab istis iam noceri potest: " as for me, I cannot any more be injured by those men "; *noceri* is here used impersonally, which is the only way in which it is possible to use the passive of a verb governing the dative. *Mihi ipsi* is the dative governed by *noceri*, and *nihil* is used adverbially, just as " nothing " was formerly in English, *e.g.* " nothing worth."

10. bonis: by the word *boni* Cicero usually designates those who were partisans of the senate; cp. *optimates.*

12. magna . . . dignitas: " great is the majesty of."

13. conscientiae: here with the same force as our word " conscience."

cum ... volent: when *cum* refers to future time, it must be followed by the future tense. The English idiom is different and less logical.

16. nullius: *nullius* and *nullo*, respectively, are used as the genitive and ablative of *nemo.*

ultro: " unchallenged."

19. qua condicione: ablative of quality. It is better in English to change the construction and translate, " what you wish to be the position of those who."

21. ad vitae fructum: by *fructus vitae* Cicero alludes to all that honour, glory, usefulness which constitute, as it were, the harvest of a citizen's life.

22. in honore vestro: Cicero had reached the highest honour which the state had it in its power to confer upon a citizen.

24. illud: explained by the *ut*-clause, *ut ea . . . ornem*, " I will certainly be careful as a private citizen to maintain and add lustre to the glory of my consulship."

25. ut: " so that."

meminerim: equivalent in meaning to a present subjunctive, just as *memini* has a present force though perfect in form.

29. curemque ut ea . . . videantur: " ensure that they seem." By my conduct hereafter, Cicero says, I will let it be seen that my achievements as consul were due, not to chance, but to my personal merit.

32. custodem huius urbis: Iupiter Optimus Maximus.

34. aeque ac priore nocte: " the same as last night."

custodiis vigiliisque: " by guards and watches "; the former word referring to the guarding of the gates, and the latter to night patrols.

FOURTH SPEECH.

Ch. I. Consult the Index for Lentulus, Vesta.

1. patres conscripti: i.e. *patres et conscripti*, " origina patricians and those enrolled or added."

3. si id depulsum sit: *sit* is subjunctive in dependence on the accusative and infinitive *vos . . . esse sollicitos.*

7. si haec condicio consulatus data est: " since the consulship has been given to me on these conditions "; *si* with the indicative here introduces a matter of fact, and has the force of " since."

10. laboribus: ablative of instrument.

vobis populoque Romano: datives with *pariatur.*

13. in quo omnis aequitas continetur: because all trials before the praetor and the iudices were held in the Forum, as the official meeting place of the Roman people.

campus: *i.e.* the Campus Martius, north-west of the city.

consularibus auspiciis: ablative of means; " by means of the auspices taken at the election of consuls." Consuls were elected by the *comitia centuriata,* which met in the Campus Martius. The divine will was consulted by means of auspices (which took the form of " observing the sky " for lightning, an unfavourable omen) on all important occasions, including the election of a magistrate. The right of " taking the auspices " was confined to patrician magistrates.

15. gentium: objective genitive. The Senate had control of foreign affairs.

lectus ad quietem datus: an allusion to the meeting of the conspirators on the night of November 6th at the house of Laeca, at which it was arranged that Cicero should be murdered at daybreak in his bed.

16. haec sedes honoris: *i.e.* the *sella curulis* or chair inlaid with ivory, on which sat curule magistrates, *i.e.* consuls, censors, praetors, and curule aediles.

17. periculo . . . insidiis: ablatives of separation with *vacua.*

multa: accusative of the external object with *tacui,* an intransitive verb used transitively by a slight stretch of its meaning. Cicero here seems to imply that he suppressed the names of some distinguished men whom he had discovered to be implicated in the plot.

18. meo quodam dolore: ablative of attendant circumstances.

19. in vestro timore: " in the case of your apprehension," *i.e.* " while only the apprehension of danger was yours."

26. subeatur: sc. *ea fortuna* as subject.

27. fatale: " marked out by fate." Lentulus was told by the soothsayers that he was destined to be the third Cornelius who should rule over Rome.

28. laeter: deliberative subjunctive.

29. prope: " if I may say so," " I may almost say," apologises for the idea, which might to Cicero's audience seem a presumptuous one.

Ch. II. Consult the Index for Allobroges, C. Gracchus, Ti. Gracchus, Memmius, Saturninus.

1. **vobis:** dative of indirect object with *consulite*. *consulo* with the dative means " to consult the interests of "; with the accusative it means " to consult."

2. **fortunas:** " property," " estates."

3. **mihi parcere:** " to show consideration for me," *i.e.* by refraining from severe punishment of the conspirators, and so lessening the hatred of their friends towards Cicero.

5. **pro eo . . . ac mereor:** these words go together, " in proportion to my deserts "; cp. the common expression *contra ac*.

mihi: dative of indirect object with *relaturos esse*.

6. **relaturos esse gratiam:** *referre gratiam* means (1) to return thanks, show gratitude, and hence (2) to reward, recompense.

7. **moriar:** future indicative.

turpis . . . immatura . . . misera: these adjectives are predicative, not attributive; " for no death can happen that is dishonourable to a brave man," etc.

8. **consulari:** " to one who has held the consulship," in Cicero's opinion the highest dignity to which mortal man could attain.

9. **ille ferreus:** " so iron-hearted a man."

11. **movear:** subjunctive in consecutive relative clause.

12. **neque . . . non . . . saepe:** " nor is it not often that," *i.e.* " nor does it infrequently happen that," " and it happens not infrequently that."

13. **exanimata:** sc. *metu*.

uxor: Terentia.

abiecta: " utterly cast down."

filia: Tullia.

parvulus filius: Marcus, then two years of age.

16. **in conspectu meo:** *i.e.* with the crowd of citizens at the doors of the temple of Concord, where the Senate was sitting. The young man had not yet attained the office of *quaestor*, in virtue of which he would become a senator; he was therefore not allowed to enter the building in which the meeting of the Senate was held.

gener: C. Calpurnius Piso, to whom Tullia was betrothed when she was only two years of age.

19. **una . . . peste:** ablative of instrument, " by the destruction which all the state must share," " in the common downfall of the state."

20. **incumbite ad salutem:** *incumbo* (lit. " to lean upon ") is often used metaphorically in the sense of " to bend one's attention to," " to devote oneself to."

21. quae impendent, nisi providetis: "which hang over you (and will burst upon you) if you do not provide against them."

22. iterum: by the time of the Gracchi it was unconstitutional to be elected tribune two years in succession.

23. voluit . . . conatus est . . . occidit: indicatives (instead of subjunctives of the causes alleged at the time of action) because the deeds referred to are represented as having been actually committed.

agrarios: "those in favour of agrarian laws," by which the *ager publicus* (state domain) was allotted to poor citizens in small holdings. Gaius Gracchus revived the Agrarian Law of his brother, which had been allowed to fall into abeyance. This revival of the Land Law of Tiberius constituted a very unimportant part of Gaius' legislation, for the bulk of the available *ager publicus* had already been allotted.

25. vestrae severitatis iudicium: "a rigorous trial before you."

27. Romae: locative with *restiterunt,* which here comes from *resto* ("to remain behind").

28. manus: "handwriting," "autographs." For the allusions in this paragraph to the conspiracy see Introduction, § 3.

29. servitia: "the class of slaves," collective use.

33. relinquatur: consecutive subjunctive; the present is used because the tense of the main verb *est initum* is primary, as it is used with present-perfect meaning.

Ch. III. Consult the Index for Allobroges, Lentulus, Volturcius.

2. multis iudiciis: "by many judicial decisions." The Senate had shown by previous decrees, on which they could not now go back, their belief in the guilt of the Catilinarians.

3. singularibus verbis: ablative of manner.

6. in custodiam: *i.e.* in the charge of various prominent men, who were held responsible for their safe keeping. This was known as *custodia libera.*

7. meo nomine: "in my honour."

8. supplicationem: "a public thanksgiving."

togato: "wearing the *toga,*" the garb of peace.

10. quae sunt omnia eius modi: lit. "all these facts are of that kind," *i.e.* "all these facts tend to show"; *modi* is genitive of quality used predicatively.

14. institui: "I have undertaken."

tamquam integrum: sc. *esset,* "as though the matter were still unjudged."

15. de facto quid iudicetis et de poena quid censeatis: *de* and the ablative is the usual construction with *referre (ad senatum); quid* *iudicetis* and *quid censeatis* are indirect questions also dependent on *referre*.

16. **consulis**: predicative genitive of the possessor; " which belong to a consul," *i.e.* " which a consul should say."

17. **nova**: with *mala*; " revolutionary evils," " the evils of revolution." Cp. *novae res*, " revolution."

21. **vobis**: so-called " dative of agent " with the gerund *statuendum*, in reality a dative of indirect object; lit. " there is a determining for you," " you must come to a decision."

ante noctem: a *decretum* of the Senate had to be passed before sunset, otherwise it was invalid, even if it was not vetoed and was accepted by the consulting magistrate.

23. **adfines**: " privy to," " involved in."

26. **multas iam provincias occupavit**: Catilina relied upon the support of debtors throughout the Roman world. Moreover, Catilina's adherent Piso (assassinated in 64 B.C.) had succeeded in making Spain disaffected towards the government, and it was suspected that P. Sittius, who commanded a mercenary army in Mauretania (which, however, was *not* a province), was privy to the conspiracy. Cicero, in order to accentuate the importance of the Senate's decision, here somewhat exaggerates.

27. **sustentando**: " by putting off," " by delaying."

Ch. IV. Consult the Index for Caesar, Silanus.

1. **sententias**: " opinions," which were elicited from individual senators by the presiding magistrate; no senator had a right to give his opinion unasked. After the debate, the presiding magistrate usually put these *sententiae* to the vote in the order in which they had been elicited; the opinions of those who had been consuls were asked for first, and were as a rule put first to the vote.

2. **censet**: " gives it as his opinion "; the question *quid censes?* was put by the presiding magistrate to each senator in an order corresponding to his official rank. See last note.

5. **in summa severitate versatur**: lit. " is busied with the utmost rigour," *i.e.* " advocates the utmost rigour."

8. **punctum**: accusative of time throughout which.

11. **usurpatum**: " practised," " employed," an entirely different meaning from that of our " usurp," which means " to occupy without right."

13. **laborum**: genitive of the remoter object, equivalent to the prepositional phrase *e laboribus*. Compare expressions like *excessus vitae = excessus e vita*.

14. **sapientes**: " philosophers," as often.

16. **sceleris**: objective genitive with *poenam*.

17. municipiis: " country towns." The inhabitants became full Roman citizens after the Social War (91–88 B.C.).

18. velis: subjunctive in hypothetical clause with impliedly indefinite subject; the condition understood is the reality of the subject.

rogare: sc. *velis.*

19. decernatur: jussive subjunctive.

20. id . . . recusare: object of *putent* and subject of *esse suae dignitatis.*

22. dignitatis: possessive genitive used as secondary predicate.

adiungit: sc. Caesar.

eorum: sc. *captivorum.*

23. horribiles custodias circumdat: either (1) " he makes their confinement a terrible (*i.e.* extremely close) one," or (2) " he surrounds them with terrible (*i.e.* ' strict ') guards." The first method of taking these words is the one usually adopted; but *custodiae* is generally used in the concrete sense, " sentinels," " guards." The *municipes* would be strict guards because of the severe penalties that would, on Caesar's motion, be imposed.

24. sancit: " he forbids under a penalty."

ne quis eorum poenam, quos condemnat . . . possit levare: the order is *ne quis possit levare poenam eorum quos condemnat;* *eorum* goes with *poenam,* not as in line 22 with *quis;* the words *eorum quos condemnat* are to be taken together, " *of* the condemned men."

25. per senatum: *i.e.* by a decree of the Senate (*senatus consultum*). A decision of the Senate, if accepted by the consulting magistrate and not vetoed by a tribune, became a *senatus consultum,* and had the force of a law.

per populum: *i.e.* by a *lex* of the *comitia centuriata* or *comitia tributa.*

27. publicari: " to be made public property," *i.e.* " to be confiscated."

29. uno dolore: instrumental ablative, " by a single pang," *i.e.* the death-pang.

31. apud inferos, etc.: the order is *illi antiqui voluerunt quaedam supplicia eius modi constituta esse impiis apud inferos.*

apud inferos: lit. " among those below," *i.e.* " in the lower world," " after death," opposed to *in vita.*

32. voluerunt: " were of opinion," " held "; *volo* often used in this sense of religious or philosophical beliefs.

33. his remotis: " if these were removed "; the ablative absolute has here a conditional force.

34. ipsam: " by itself."

Ch. V. Consult Index for Caesar, Lentulus.

1. **mea video quid intersit:** *mea* belongs to *interest*, but is put first for the sake of emphasis. In the phrase *mea refert* the possessive adjective *mea* probably agrees with *re*, the original sense having been " it bears in the direction of my affairs." If this view is correct, *interest* in the phrase *mea interest* is merely an imitation of the construction of *refert* in *mea refert*.

3. **popularis:** " democratic "; the *populares* endeavoured to overthrow the now effete and incompetent government of the *optimates*, or aristocratic party. The party called *populares* included both moderate reformers and revolutionists like Catilina. The constant struggle between democrats and oligarchs was destined ultimately to culminate in the military monarchy of the Caesars.

4. **hoc:** sc. *Caesare.*

cognitore: a *cognitor* was one who made himself thoroughly familiar with a civil case and then acted as representative or advocate of either the plaintiff or the defendant.

6. **nescio an . . . contrahatur:** *an* sometimes introduces apparently single dependent questions after expressions of doubt; in such sentences it is always the *probable* alternative that is expressed; thus *nescio an* is to be rendered by " I am inclined to think " or " probably," not by " I do not know whether."

negotii: partitive genitive with *amplius.*

7. **tamen:** " in any case," *i.e.* whichever of the two proposals you adopt.

periculorum: objective genitive with *rationes,* " considerations."

8. **habemus enim:** " we have then," etc.

9. **amplitudo:** " greatness," " dignity." The *gens Iulia* was one of the oldest of the patrician clans.

11. **intellectum est:** sc. *a Caesare*; " Caesar has realised the difference," etc.

contionatorum: properly those who speak at *contiones*, or public meetings which magistrates had the right of convening as a preliminary to legislation, etc. None but magistrates or citizens introduced by them were allowed to speak: the people could only hear and acclaim; but the *contio* was a thoroughly democratic institution, and as it was often used for the purpose of stirring up the populace, the word *contionator* came to mean " demagogue," " political agitator."

13. **istis:** *i.e.* senators who belonged to the " Liberal " or democratic party.

15. **non neminem:** " many a one," " several."

ne de capite, etc.: according to the laws, questions affecting the *caput* of a Roman citizen could not be decided by the Senate or by any other body except the Roman people or its delegates the commission courts. But the Senate by means of the *senatus decretum ultimum* (see Introduction, § 5) claimed the right of investing the consuls with full powers of life and death. *Caput* was not only the " life " or " right to live " of a Roman citizen, but also all the other rights that he possessed, viz. liberty, citizenship, and family rights. By the Lex Porcia (197 B.C.) it was enacted that the only capital punishment that could be inflicted on a Roman citizen was that of exile, which involved loss of citizenship. Thus it will be seen that in deciding on the death of the conspirators the Senate passed a sentence which could not even be passed by the *comitia*, which was in law the only judge on the *caput* of a citizen.

16. nudius tertius: = *nunc dies tertius est;* " the day before yesterday."

17. dedit . . . decrevit: "*voted* for giving . . . *joined* in the decree."

18. iam hoc, etc.: *hoc* refers to *quid . . . iudicarit;* after *quid* supply *ille* as antecedent of *qui.*

19. quaesitori: "the examining magistrate"; generally used of the praetor who presided in criminal trials (*quaestiones*), but here applied by Cicero to himself, since as consul he had conducted the preliminary investigation against the conspirators.

gratulationem: " a vote of thanks."

21. at vero C. Caesar, etc.: *i.e.* Caesar had in his speech appealed to the various laws which provide for an appeal to the people in cases affecting *caput*; but he cannot consistently hold that these laws affect the case at issue, otherwise he would not be recognising the jurisdiction of the Senate by taking part in the present trial.

legem Semproniam: a plebiscite passed by Gaius Gracchus in 122 B.C., which reinforced the earlier laws (*e.g.* the *lex Valeria*, 509 B.C.) securing the right of appeal. The Sempronian plebiscite provided *ne de capite civium Romanorum iniussu populi iudicaretur*, " that no trial should be held on the *caput* (legal right) of a citizen without the consent of the people." See note on l. 14 above, and Introduction, § 5.

22. qui autem rei publicae sit hostis, eum civem nullo modo esse posse: Cicero is here guilty of the fallacy of begging the question, or arguing in a circle: it was just this declaration of a citizen as a *hostis* by the Senate that was forbidden by the Sempronian plebiscite and its predecessors; a citizen could be made a *hostis* only after he had been tried and convicted by a court of law, and this court of law must be formed by the *populus*, not by the Senate.

23. sit: subjunctive in dependence on the accusative and infinitive phrase *eum . . . posse.*

24. latorem: C. Gracchus.

iniussu populi: this fact by no means strengthens Cicero's argument; it only shows that the Senate, by passing the *senatus consultum ultimum,* in virtue of which the consul Opimius with armed slaves

and senators hunted C. Gracchus to death (121 B.C.), were simply
law-breakers; for it is beyond question that after the passing of the
Sempronian plebiscite the Senate's *decretum ultimum*, investing the
consuls with dictatorial rights, became illegal.

24. rei publicae: dative with *dependisse.*

27. etiam: of time, " still," " any more."

30. in posterum: " as regards the future."

supplicio levando: ablative of means.

31. se iactare: " to get a cheap advertisement."

in perniciem: *in* with the accusative often denotes aim or
object.

Ch. VI. Consult the Index for Allobroges, L. Caesar, Cassius,
Cethegus, Gabinius, Gracchus, Lentulus, Silanus, Vesta.

1. sive . . . sive: " if on the one hand . . . if on the other."

2. comitem ad contionem: for *contio* see note on Ch. V., l. 11. By
comes Caesar, the democratic leader, is referred to. A magistrate
holding a *contio* could introduce any citizens to the assembly, that
they might express their views. Those who were thus introduced
(*deducti in contionem*) were generally political leaders who happened
not to be magistrates at the time.

populo: with *carum atque iucundum.*

5. obtinebo: " I will maintain."

8. ita . . . ut: this use in asseverations or adjurations of *ita* with
a jussive subjunctive (here *liceat*), answered by *ut* with the indicative,
is not uncommon, especially in the expression *ita di me ament, ut,*
" so help me God, as I," etc. " So may it be allowed me to enjoy
. . . as I am not influenced," etc.

12. mihi: dative of person judging with *videor.*

14. animo: ablative of instrument.

sepulta: " buried in ruins."

15. aspectus . . . et furor: a hendiadys, " furious look."

17. regnantem: " ruling as a king "; the title of *rex* was peculiarly
odious to the Roman people, in whose minds it was associated with
the tyranny of the Tarquins and the life and death struggle for
republican liberty.

18. purpuratum: lit. " clad in purple "; when used as a substantive the word denotes a " high officer " at an oriental court, a
" grandvizier."

20. matrum: subjective genitive with *lamentationem.*

familias: archaic form of the genitive singular; the form *familiae*
is also often found.

21. Vestalium: objective genitive with *vexationem.* For the Vestal
Virgins or Vestals see Index *s.v.* Vesta.

mihi: sc. *videtur esse;* the dative is one of person judging.

29. importunus: (1) " unsuited "; hence (2) " irksome," " trouble-some "; hence, of persons, (3) " harsh," " oppressive," " brutal."
nocentis: objective genitive.

30. lenierit: subjunctive in a relative clause implying cause.
in: " in the case of."

33. rei publicae: genitive of definition or material, expressing that in which the *domicilium* consists.

34. qui id egerunt ut: " who made it their object that."

35. deflagrati: lit. " burnt down," *i.e.* " utterly destroyed."

37. in: " in the case of," " in the matter of."

38. nisi vero: an ironical expression; lit. " unless indeed." Trans-late " but perhaps." It is implied that the statement introduced by " *nisi vero* " is an absurd one.
L. Caesar: see Index of Proper Names.

41. sororis suae . . . virum: P. Lentulus the conspirator, who married Julia, sister of L. Caesar, widow of M. Antonius Creticus, and by him mother of M. Antonius the triumvir.

42. cum avum suum . . . dixit: this has the force of an explanatory present participle—" informing the house that his own grandfather," etc.

avum: M. Fulvius Flaccus, for whom see Index *s.v.* Fulvius.

43. consulis: L. Opimius, for whom see Index.

45. quorum quod simile factum: lit. " of whom what deed was like those ? " *i.e.* " what deed did they do like those of the conspirators ? "
quorum: Fulvius Flaccus and his leader C. Gracchus.

simile: sc. *factis coniuratorum.*

factum: a substantive. Cicero's view here is not shared by many modern historians of Rome. C. Gracchus wished to rule Rome as an annually re-elected tribune by means of the plebeian *concilium,* just as Pericles had ruled Athens as an annually re-elected general by means of the Athenian assembly.

initum: sc. *est.*

delendae rei publicae: objective genitive of the gerundive, depending on *consilium.*

46. largitionis: the reference is to the *lex frumentaria* (corn law) of C. Gracchus, by which corn was distributed to the city mob at less than half the average price. This distribution formed a pernicious precedent.

47. partium: subjective genitive. C. Gracchus transferred the jury courts (which heard cases against provincial governors) to the Knights or *equites,* and so created a new *ordo equester* inimical to the ruling oligarchy of the Senate.

48. huius avus Lentuli: Publius Cornelius Lentulus, who sup-ported Opimius in his attack on the Aventine, which was occupied by C. Gracchus and Fulvius Flaccus. C. Gracchus fled and committed suicide (121 b.c.).

50. de summa re publica: "from the fabric of the state in its entirety"; these words are the antithesis of *fundamenta reipublicae* (l. 51).

51. servitia: " slaves," abstract for concrete.

55. vereamini: jussive subjunctive in semi-dependence on *censeo*. The verb has an ironical force.

57. quam: adverb, " than."

Ch. VII. **1. exaudio:** " I hear distinctly." The senators were making remarks to one another, and these remarks reached Cicero's ears.

dissimulare: to pretend that a thing does not exist when it really does exist, " to conceal," " to ignore." *Simulare* means to pretend that a thing exists when it really does not exist, " to pretend," " to simulate."

2. voces: " remarks," " expressions."

6. cum . . . tum: " both . . . and," " not only . . . but also."

9. ordinum: referring especially to the *ordo senatorius* and the *ordo equester*. The *ordo nobilum* consisted of those patricians and wealthy plebeians whose ancestors had held curule office; it was practically identical with the *ordo senatorius*. Other *ordines* were formed by the *tribuni aerarii* and the *scribae* (see below, ll. 29 and 30). *Ordinum*, *generum*, and *aetatum* are genitives of quality or description.

11. forum: see note on Ch. I., l. 12.

12. templi ac loci: hendiadys, " sacred spot."

post urbem conditam: " since the foundation of the city." A substantive and a perfect participle passive often together form a phrase concrete in form but abstract in meaning, expressing an action performed on the substantive.

13. sentirent: subjunctive in consecutive relative clause; *in qua* is equivalent to *talis ut in ea*, " such that in it."

17. civium . . . hostium: genitives of definition or material, denoting that in which a thing consists, with *numero*, which here means " class," " category."

20. equites Romanos: the *equites* formed the second grade after the senators, and served originally as cavalry. They were now an upper middle class of capitalists. Their interests were wholly material and commercial; hence their great aim was to secure a strong and stable government and to prevent revolution. Thus they took sides sometimes with the *populares* against the weak and incompetent rule of the oligarchs, and sometimes with the *optimates* against revolutionary designs such as those of Catilina. Their

influence was generally sufficient to turn the scale in favour of the
party on whose side they declared themselves.

commemorem: deliberative subjunctive.

21. ita . . . ut: " only so far . . . that," " indeed . . . but yet ";
ut . . . certent here restricts or limits the statement in the principal
clause.

ordinis: genitive of relation, a variety of the objective genitive;
the genitive is here almost equivalent to *de* and the ablative.

consilii: either " right of being consulted " (by magistrates),
" right of deliberation," or " wisdom," " counsel."

23. ex: " after."

annorum: genitive of quality with *dissensione*.

dissensione: in 121 B.C. the jury-courts, of which the most
important was the Commission which tried provincial governors for
extortion, were transferred from the Senate to the *equites*; this was
the beginning of the enmity between the knights and the senators,
since the senatorial governors were now practically controlled by the
knights, although dishonest governors, in return for a share of the
plunder of the provinces, connived at the peculations of the equestrian tax-farmers, and were therefore acquitted, when charged with
extortion, by the equestrian courts. In 81 B.C. Sulla restored the
jury-courts to the Senate; but corrupt senatorial governors were
always acquitted by a senatorial court; and finally in 70 B.C., by
the *Lex Aurelia*, a compromise was effected, and the jury-courts were
composed of three panels, one of senators, one of knights, and one
of *tribuni aerarii* (for whom see note on l. 29 below).

ordinis: genitive of relation, or of the remoter object, a variety of
the objective genitive, with *dissensione*. *Dissensio ordinis* = the
prepositional phrase *dissensio ab ordine*.

24. concordiam: the great ideal of Cicero was to save the constitution
by uniting the propertied classes in defence of the senatorial government. But he only succeeded in bringing about a temporary
alliance which bolstered up the constitution for a time. The
senatorial oligarchy was essentially weak and incompetent, and a
military despotism was, sooner or later, inevitable.

30. tribunos aerarios: originally tribal officers who collected the
war-tax (*tributum*) from the tribes and were responsible for the pay
(*aes*, hence *aerarii*) of the troops; the *Lex Aurelia* (see note on l. 23)
gave them a share in the jury-courts, and henceforth they formed a
new *ordo*, ranking next to the *ordo equester* and consisting of all who
had more than 300,000 but less than 400,000 sesterces.

scribas item universos: sc. *convenisse video*. The *scribae* were
permanent public clerks, who also formed an *ordo*; a certain number
were assigned to each quaestor, aedile, and tribune of the plebs.
Those belonging to the quaestors were the most distinguished; they
were exclusively *ingenui* (freemen), while those of other magistrates
were usually *libertini* (freedmen).

30. **cum**: concessive, " although."

31. **hic dies**: the Nones of December (December 5th); on this day the quaestors entered upon their office and were assigned by lot to their several departments; and the *scribae* drew lots to decide to what magistrates they were to be attached.

aerarium: the public treasury was in the temple of Saturn, near the temple of Concord, and here the drawing of lots by the quaestors and the *scribae* took place.

frequentasset: probably potential, " would have brought together in great numbers."

36. **sit**: subjunctive in consecutive relative clause, introduced by *cui* (= *ut ei*); *cum* does not go with *sit*, but corresponds to *tum*, " not only . . . but also."

Ch. VIII. Consult the Index for Lentulus.

1. **operae pretium est**: " it is worth while," lit. " it is the price of (one's) labour." *Operae* is a subjective genitive.

3. **sua virtute**: " by their own merits "; manumission was often a reward of good service.

fortunam huius civitatis: lit. " the good fortune consisting in this citizenship," *i.e.* " the privilege of our citizenship "; *civitatis* is genitive of definition or that in which a thing consists.

10. **qui . . . sit . . . qui . . . perhorrescat**: we have here two consecutive relative clauses; the first restricts the meaning of *servus*, the second is an ordinary consecutive clause, in which *qui* = *ut is*.

11. **haec**: " all that is before our eyes "; Cicero by a sweep of his hand indicates the buildings in the Forum.

stare: " to stand unharmed."

12. **voluntatis**: genitive of divided whole (or " partitive " genitive) with *tantum*.

13. **hoc quod auditum est**: " this rumour."

lenonem: lit. " a pimp," " a pander," hence " a vile agent."

15. **tabernas**: " small shops "; these were simply wooden booths.
pretio: ablative of instrument with *sollicitari*.

16. **imperitorum**: as we would say " uneducated people."

17. **fortuna . . . voluntate**: ablatives of cause; *voluntate* means " their own will," " their own action," or perhaps " their own (evil) desires."

18. **illum ipsum . . . locum**: *i.e.* the Forum, to which Cicero would point.

sellae . . . operis . . . quaestus: genitives of description or definition.

19. **lectulum**: this does not mean " a small bed "; the diminutive here conveys the notion of comfort, " his cosy bed."

20. otiosum: *i.e.* untroubled by revolution.

22. immo vero: " yes indeed," " I should rather say." *Immo* (often strengthened by *vero*) is used to contradict or qualify what precedes.

24. instrumentum: " stock-in-trade," the means by which a man carries on his work or trade; his " tools," " goods," or " capital " in the wider sense.

25. quorum: *i.e. eorum qui in tabernis sunt.*

26. occlusis tabernis: ablative absolute used causally.

incensis: sc. *tabernis*; the ablative absolute is here used conditionally, and the protasis of *futurum fuit* is implied in it; *incensis = si incensae essent.*

fuit: not *fuisset*, since the verb *sum* accompanied by a gerund, gerundive, or (as here) by a future participle, and the verbs *possum, debeo, oportet, decet, necesse est* (which imply duty or necessity) are put in the indicative instead of in the subjunctive in the apodosis of conditional clauses in which the condition is unfulfilled.

Ch. IX. Consult the Index for Vesta.

7. impiae: since the ties of *pietas*, or patriotism, are broken; " of unpatriotic men."

9. arcem et Capitolium: the Capitoline hill consisted of two heights; the northern height was called the *Arx* (Citadel), the south-west height was the *Capitolium*; on it was built the great temple of Capitoline Jove.

10. Penatium: the Penates were gods of the household, and of the State as a union of households. They had a temple on the Velia, a ridge of the Palatine.

ignem illum Vestae: the temple of Vesta was on the south-east side of the Forum and was well in view from the temple of Concord; hence *illum*, " yonder."

13. fortunis: " estates," " property."

17. facultas: " opportunity," " advantage "; the word is attracted into the clause of its relative.

18. in civili causa: " in a case where politics are concerned."

22. una nox: either that on which the envoys of the Allobroges left Rome, or that on which the conspirators met at Laeca's house.

23. delerit: = *deleverit;* subjunctive in indirect question. The whole expression is a concise form of *cogitate quantis laboribus fundatum sit* (subjunctive in indirect question) *imperium, quanta virtute stabilita sit libertas, quanta deorum benignitate auctae exaggerataeque sint fortunae quae omnia una nox delevit.*

non modo: used for *non modo non* when the predicate is common to both clauses.

28. functa: sc. *esse.*

Ch. X. Consult the Index for Marius, Numantia, Paullus, Perses, Pompeius, and Scipio (1) and (2).

1. ad sententiam: sc. *rogandam.* The presiding magistrate (here Cicero as consul) questioned the members separately as to their views *(sententiae)*, beginning with *consulares* and ending with ex-quaestors and private members. At the end of the debate the president put the *sententiae* to the vote one after another, usually in the order in which he had elicited them. Since the debate was not yet over, and several members had still to be asked for their opinion, *rogare sententiam* here means not " to put the question to the vote " (as it is sometimes rendered), but " to ask members for their opinions."

5. furore et scelere: hendiadys, " criminal fury."

9. quam . . . mihi . . . minitantur: *minor* and *minitor* are constructed either (1) as here, with accusative of thing and dative of person, or (2) with accusative and infinitive.

omnibus est parata: " is prepared for all," *i.e.* " is the ultimate lot of all."

10. vitae: objective genitive with *laudem.*

tantam laudem quanta: lit. " so much praise, by how much," *i.e.* " so much praise as that by which."

12. reipublicae: genitive of the remoter object, corresponding to the prepositional phrase *de republica.* Some read *conservata republica* (ablative absolute).

13. ille: a demonstrative adjective, " the great." For Scipio Africanus Maior see Index *s.v.* Scipio (1); and for Scipio Africanus Minor see Index *s.v.* Scipio (2).

16. Carthaginem: see Index *s.v.* Scipio (1) and (2).

18. currum: " triumphal car," *i.e.* " triumph."

19. gloria: ablative of description.

20. obsidione: " armed occupation."

21. Pompeius: see Index.

22. quibus solis cursus: sc. *continetur.*

23. loci: partitive genitive with *aliquid.*

24. nostrae gloriae: = *nostri gloriae,* where *nostri* is objective genitive, depending on the dative *gloriae.*

25. possimus: subjunctive in relative final clause *(quo = ut eo).* So *revertantur* in l. 26.

27. uno loco: " in one point," " in one respect."

condicio: " terms," hence " position," " circumstances."

29. recepti: i.e. *in fidem.*

32. possis: potential subjunctive with indefinite subject; lit. " you would not be able " (if you were to try), " you can never."

39. quae: = *ut ea,* with consecutive subjunctive *(possit* in l. 41).

Ch. XI. 1. pro imperio: " in place of the military command."
All higher magistrates held the *imperium* (" right to command "),
but it was only beyond the borders of Italy that they could exercise
the full military authority. In Italy the *imperium* was restricted
to civil jurisdiction. Sulla (81 B.C.) had divorced the civil from the
military authority by enacting that consuls and praetors should
discharge civil functions during their year of office at Rome, and
should then become governors of provinces as proconsuls or pro-
praetors with full military authority.

pro provincia quam neglexi: " in place of the province which I
have relinquished." By the *Lex Sempronia* of 122 B.C. it was
enacted that the Senate determine which should be consular provinces
before the election of the consuls who were to hold them.   Then the
consuls, when elected, settled between themselves by lot or by
arrangement which of the two provinces nominated by the Senate
each should take. The provinces for the consuls of 63 B.C. (which
they would enter upon in January 62 B.C.) were Macedonia and
Cisalpine Gaul. Since Macedonia was a lucrative province, Cicero
bought up his colleague Antonius, who was in debt and had shown
himself favourable to the designs of Catilina, by relinquishing it to
him. He afterwards resigned Cisalpine Gaul, so that at the end of
his year of office he had no province to go to, no army to command,
and no chance of a triumph.

2. laudis: objective genitive.

4. pro clientelis hospitiisque provincialibus: clientship   was
originally the intimate and reciprocal duties of attachment and
interest based on the private relations at Rome between the patricians and their clients, who were freedmen or refugees.   The
patricians were called *patroni* and had to protect the client and
represent him in the law courts in return for personal services.   In
later times provincials, and often whole provinces, asked their former
governor to be their *patronus*, and as such he was bound to look
after their interests in return for hospitality and friendship.

5. urbanis opibus: " by means of political influence exercised in
the city."

6. pro meis . . . studiis: " in return for my zeal "; *pro* in the
preceding sentences means " in place of "; here it means " in return
for."

15. solius: genitive to agree with the genitive of the personal
pronoun understood from *suo*.

20. decernite diligenter, ut instituistis: here as in Ch. X., l. 1, the
reference is to the *sententiae* or opinions elicited by the presiding
magistrate from individual members of the Senate, not to the putting
of the question to the vote. Translate " Give your views deliber-
ately, as you have begun to do " (with reference to the *sententiae* of
Silanus and Caesar).

23. per se ipsum praestare: " to be personally responsible for."

INDEX OF PROPER NAMES.

A.

Ahāla, -ae, m.: Gaius Servilius Ahala was Master of Horse to the Dictator Lucius Cincinnatus in 439 B.C. He summoned Spurius Maelius to appear before the dictator, and at the latter's bidding slew Maelius in the Forum when he refused to appear. Ahala was brought to trial subsequently, but escaped the consequences of condemnation in the usual way by going into exile. See below, Maelius.

Allobrŏges, -um, m.: a powerful people of Gaul, dwelling to the east of the Rhone, and chiefly between that river and the Isère. They were conquered by Quintus Fabius Maximus, 121 B.C., but did not rest contented under Roman rule. The part they played in the Catilinarian Conspiracy is explained in the Introduction, p. 11.

Apūlĭa, -ae, f.: a district in south-east Italy, north of Calabria, and east of Samnium.

Aurēlia Via: a military road along the coast of Etruria as far as Pisae and Luna; it was continued by the *Via Aemilia* of Scaurus to Genua, 109 B.C.

C.

Caesar, -ăris, m.: (1) Gaius Julius Caesar, born in 100 B.C., was from his earliest days an opponent of the senatorial party. His name was placed on the lists of the proscribed during Sulla's reign of terror (82 B.C.), and he had to quit Italy; in 78 he came back and won the position of popular leader by dint of the most lavish expenditure, private and public. In 63 he was made Pontifex Maximus. He has been suspected of complicity in Catilina's plot; but this is not likely. At any rate, in the debate in the Senate concerning the punishment of the conspirators, he advocated lenient measures. In 62 he was praetor, in 60 he formed with Pompeius and Crassus the coalition known as the First Triumvirate, and in 59 he was consul. For the next ten years Caesar was engaged in his province of Gaul, which he completely subdued. The account of his campaigns there, with his two invasions of Britain, he gives in the *De Bello Gallico*. In 49 the jealousy of Pompeius led to the Civil War. Having defeated Pompeius at the battle of Pharsalia (84), and crushed all remaining opposition by the victories of Thapsus (46) and Munda (45), he was made Dictator for life. On the Ides of March, 44 B.C., he was assassinated by some of his personal friends, notably Brutus and Cassius. (2) Lucius Julius Caesar, surnamed Strabo: consul in 64 B.C. His sister Julia was the wife of Lentulus the conspirator. His mother Fulvia was a daughter of Fulvius Flaccus, the adherent of Gaius Gracchus.

Cassius, -i, m.: Lucius Cassius Longinus, of unknown descent, was a candidate for the consulship of 63 B.C., along with Cicero. He became a confederate of Catilina, but escaped when Lentulus and the others were executed; in his absence he was condemned to death, but his ultimate fate is unknown. He was of senatorial rank. His part in the conspiracy was to be the firing of the city.

Cătĭlīna, -ae, m.: see Introduction, pp. 8–12.

Cotta, -ae, m.: Lucius Aurelius Cotta was consul 65 B.C., with Lucius Manlius Torquatus, in the place of the consuls elected for the year, who were disqualified on account of bribery.

E.

Etrūrĭa, -ae, f.: the country of the Etrusci or Tusci, called by the Greeks Tyrrhēni. It extended from the right bank of the Tiber northwards to the Apennines. The early Etruscans were probably a mixed race of immigrants; their real origin cannot be conclusively traced. They were a highly civilised and powerful people when Rome was in her infancy, and only succumbed to the rising power of the latter after more than a hundred years of warfare. They received the Roman franchise in 91 B.C. In the civil war Etruria sided with Marius against Sulla, and was consequently regarded by Catilina as a favourable centre for his military operations. Faesŭlae (now *Fiesole*) became his headquarters, the *Manliana castra* that Cicero frequently alludes to.

F.

Faesŭlae, -arum, f.: see Etruria.

Flaccus, -i, m.: Lucius Valerius Flaccus, one of the praetors in 63 B.C., assisted Cicero in obtaining the evidence of the Allobroges against the conspirators (III. § 5.) In 59 he was successfully defended by Cicero from a charge of extortion brought against him by the Asiatic provincials, he having proceeded to that province as *propraetor* in 62 B.C.

Fŏrum Aurēlĭum: now *Mont-alto*, a little place near the coast of Etruria, on the Aurelian Way, about fifty miles from Rome. Like many places with similar names, it was probably in the beginning a gathering-place, or canteen, for the workmen employed in constructing the road.

Fulvĭus, -i, m.: Marcus Fulvius Flaccus was consul in 125 B.C., and tribune of the people three years later, and a partisan of Gaius

Gracchus. In the attack made by the consul Opimius on the latter (112 B.C.), Fulvius fought for his party, and was killed together with his elder son. The younger, who had been sent with terms of reconciliation to Opimius before the fighting began, was thrown into prison and murdered. See below, Gracchus and Opimius.

Fūrius, -i, m.: Publius Furius, one of the conspirators, who effected his escape.

G.

Găbīnius, -ii, m.: Gaius Gabinius Cimber, an accomplice of Catilina, was consigned, after the discovery of the conspiracy, to the custody of M. Crassus and executed. His name is given by Sallust as Publius Gabinius Capito.

Gallīa, -ae, f.: the general name for the country inhabited by the Galli or Celtae. The two great divisions of the country are: (1) *Gallia Transalpina*, corresponding to modern France, and (2) *Gallia Cisalpina*, comprising the northern portion of Italy above Liguria, Etruria, and Umbria up to the Alps.

Gallīcus Ager: a strip of coast land in Umbria, between the Rubicon and the Aesis. It was occupied by the Senonian Gauls about 400 B.C.; they were exterminated in 283 B.C., and in 232 B.C. their territory was allotted to citizen colonists.

Glaucīa, -ae, m.: Gaius Servilius Glaucia was a leader of the popular party, whose services Marius employed to assist him in securing the consulship for the sixth time (100 B.C.). Glaucia, however, with his associate, Saturninus, became unpopular, owing to their excesses, and had to seek refuge in the Capitol. Marius tried to save them by putting them for safety in the Senate-house; but the senatorial party was too strong to be controlled, and put them both to death.

Gracchus, -i, m.: the two famous brothers were sons of Tiberius Sempronius Gracchus (*clarissimus pater*), who was consul in 177 B.C. and again fourteen years later; he held other high offices, and won great credit for pacifying Spain and subduing Sardinia. His wife, the celebrated Cornelia, was daughter of P. Scipio Africanus Major, the conqueror of Hannibal. The elder brother, Tiberius, was tribune in 133 B.C., when he brought forward a vigorous agrarian law and other kindred measures of reform. The senators, headed by Scipio Nasīca, took up arms, attacked the people, and killed Gracchus, in about the thirty-fifth year of his age. The younger brother, Gaius Sempronius Gracchus, became tribune in 123, and again in 122. He revived and considerably extended his brother's proposals, and carried them, thereby greatly curtailing the power and privileges of the senatorial order. The latter by various underhand schemes undermined the power of Gracchus, then openly attacked him and his party in the Forum, when they appeared there to oppose retrogressive

legislation. Gracchus refused to take up arms, and was slain
(121 B.C.) with about three thousand others. See Fulvius, Opimius,
and Scipio.

I.

Iuppĭter, Iŏvis, m.: called Stator as staying the flight of the
Romans in battle, and generally establishing the existing order of
things. His temple on the Palatine Mount was, according to the
early legend, dedicated by Romulus, the first king of Rome, in consequence of a vow made in battle against the Sabines. Hence he is
described as *antiquissimus custos* of Rome and things Roman.

L.

Laeca, -ae, m.: Marcus Porcius Laeca, a senator and conspirator
with Catilina. In his house *inter falcarios* took place the meeting
of November 6th, when Catilina made his final arrangements.

Lentŭlus, -i, m.: (1) Publius Cornelius Lentulus, the chief accomplice of Catilina, was a member of a patrician family, who attained
to the consulship in 71 B.C. His life was so infamous that he was
expelled from the Senate, 70 B.C.: he became in his disgrace a
dangerous man, and was ready to join any enterprise which might
give him hope of vengeance. When Catilina left the city, Lentulus
assumed the direction of the affairs of the conspirators, and his
letter to Catilina is written in the tone of a superior to his subordinate. Indeed, he went so far as to declare that the fates had
predicted the mastery of the city to himself. His ability was,
however, unequal to his pretensions; and his want of energy, and
especially his infatuation in placing confidence in the fickle Gauls,
resulted in the collapse of the whole plot. He was executed in the
Tullianum. (2) Publius Cornelius Lentulus, grandfather of (1); he
supported the consul Opimius in his attack upon C. Gracchus and
his adherents (121 B.C.).

Lĕpĭdus, -i, m.: (1) Manius Aemilius Lepidus was consul with
Tullus in the year 66 B.C., when Catilina formed his earlier plot. He
belonged to the party of the *optimates*, but practically retired from
politics when the civil war broke out in 49 B.C. (2) Manius Aemilius
Lepidus, consul 78 B.C., endeavoured to overthrow the Sullan
Constitution, but was defeated by his colleague, Q. Lutatius Catulus,
and retired to Sardinia, where he died (77 B.C.).

M.

Maelĭus, -i, m.: Spurius Maelius, according to the legend, was a
rich plebeian, who during the great famine of the year 439 B.C.
bought up corn and distributed it at a nominal price among the

poorer classes; he was accordingly accused of aspiring to kingly power, and was put to death. See above, Ahala.

Manlĭus, -i, m.: Gaius Manlius served as a centurion under Sulla; and in consequence of his military experience he was made the leader of the military side of the conspiracy. He hoisted the standard of revolt in Etruria (October 27th), and fortified the camp at Faesulae.

Marcellus, -i, m.: Marcus Marcellus was consul in the year 51 B.C. and an intimate friend of Cicero's. He was best known as a bitter opponent of Julius Caesar, but withdrew from the civil war after the battle of Pharsalus (48 B.C.) to Mytilēne, where he studied philosophy. His relatives at Rome procured his pardon; and Cicero's speech of thanks to Caesar is still extant. He was, however, murdered at Athens on his way home.

Marĭus, -i, m.: Gaius Marius, the great soldier, was born at Arpinum in 157 B.C. He distinguished himself greatly at the siege of Numantia, in Spain (134 B.C.), conquered Jugurtha, king of Numidia (105 B.C.), and by a victory over the Teutons at Aquae Sextiae (102 B.C.) in his fourth consulate, and by another over the Cimbrians at Vercellae in his fifth, in the following year, saved Italy from being overrun by barbarian hordes. In 100 B.C. he was consul again, and had to crush by force of arms the outbreak of the demagogues Saturninus and Glaucia, whose aid had made him consul. He served in the Social War (90–88 B.C.), but the command in the Mithradatic war (88 B.C.) was given to his rival Sulla, who drove him into temporary exile. In the absence of Sulla in the East, Marius returned, joined Cinna, who meanwhile had led the democratic party, and effected an entry into Rome (87 B.C.), and massacred his opponents. He proclaimed himself and Cinna consuls for the ensuing year, but died on the eighteenth day of this, his seventh consulship.

Massilĭa, -ae, f.: now Marseilles; it was a free Greek state, an ally of Rome, and a favourite refuge for political exiles from Rome.

Memmius, -i, m.: Gaius Memmius was originally a bitter democrat, and vehemently attacked the corrupt policy of the Senate at the beginning of the Jugurthine War (112–111 B.C.). He afterwards went over to the side of the Government, and in 100 B.C. he was a candidate in opposition to Glaucia for the consulship of 99 B.C., and was murdered at the instigation of Glaucia during the consular elections.

Mĕtellus, -i, m.: (1) Quintus Caecilius Metellus Celer was praetor in the year 63 B.C. and consul three years later. He took an active part against Catilina, and prevented him from breaking out of Etruria into Gaul. He died in 59 B.C., according to popular report, from poison given by his profligate wife Clodia. (2) A Marcus Metellus mentioned (I., § 19, if the reading is correct) as the man with whom Catilina was placed in *libera custodia* is not otherwise known.

N.

Numantia, -ae, f.: now Guarray, a town in Spain on the Upper Douro, belonging to the Arevaci. It held out for twelve years against the power of Rome, and it was only after a severe struggle that it was captured by Scipio Aemilianus in 133 B.C. The fall of Numantia broke down the national resistance of Spain.

O.

Octāvius, -ii, m.: Gnaeus Octavius, consul with Cinna, 87 B.C. He defeated and drove Cinna from the city, when the latter endeavoured to act in the interests of the fugitive Marius.

Ŏpīmĭus, -i, m.: Lucius Opimius was consul in the year 121 B.C., and a violent opponent of Gaius Gracchus. Being invested by senatorial decree with supreme powers, Opimius with an armed force slew Gracchus, Fulvius, and many of their adherents. In 109 B.C. he was convicted of having taken bribes three years previously from the Numidian king Jugurtha, and fled as an exile to Dyrrhachium in Epirus, where he died in great misery. See also Gracchus and Fulvius above.

P.

Pălătĭum, -i, n.: the Palatium, or Mons Palatīnus, the central hill of the seven hills of Rome, was the site of the original city. In later days it was covered with important buildings, public and private. On its northern slope was the temple of Iuppiter Stator, looking over the Forum. Cicero's house was on the N.E. edge. Near it was the house of the orator Hortensius, which afterwards became the imperial residence of Augustus and his successors, and was called the Palatium. Hence our word " palace."

Paulus, -i, m.: Lucius Aemilius Paulus served with success in Spain, 189 B.C. He was consul in 181 B.C.; but his chief title to fame was his defeat of the Macedonian king Perseus or Perses at Pydna in South Macedonia in 168 B.C. This battle decided the fate of Greece, and finally secured for Rome the supremacy of the world. See under *Perses*.

Perses, -ae, m.: Perses or Perseus, the last king of Macedonia, (179–168 B.C.). In spite of the great resources of Macedonia and some initial successes, his cowardice and weakness of character were so great that he abandoned his impregnable fortifications at the gates of Macedonia (169), and was compelled by Aemilius Paulus to retreat to Pydna, where he was utterly defeated in 168 B.C. (see under Paulus). Macedonia was then split up into four republics.

Pĭcēnum, -i, n.: a strip of land on the coast of the Adriatic between Ancona and Pescara, bounded on the north and west by Umbria and Sabinum, and on the south by the lands of the Vestini.

Pompēĭus, -i, m.: Gnaeus Pompeius, surnamed Magnus, was born in 106 B.C. After a brilliant success in the First Civil War (83–71 B.C.) he allied himself with the democratic party, and as consul in 70 B.C. overthrew the oligarchic constitution of Sulla. In 67 the *Lex Gabinia* invested him with extraordinary powers in the Mediterranean, by means of which he subdued the Cilician pirates, who were ruining Roman trade; and in 66 B.C. the Lex Manilia gave him the command against Mithradates, king of Pontus, who threatened Roman Asia. He conquered Mithradates and reorganised the East, making the Euphrates the boundary and forming the new provinces of Syria, Bithynia-Pontus, and Crete. He returned to Rome in 62 B.C., and formed with Julius Caesar and Crassus the First Triumvirate in 60 B.C. But he soon became jealous of Caesar, and after 55 he drifted away from the alliance with him, finally taking up the cause of the Senate against Caesar and the democratic party in 52 B.C., when he was made sole consul. In 49 B.C., when Caesar crossed the Rubicon and marched on Rome, Pompeius retired to Greece, where at Pharsalus in 48 B.C. he was severely defeated. He then fled to Egypt, where he was killed.

Pomptīnus, -i, m.: Gaius Pomptinus took part in the Servile War, 71 B.C. He was praetor in 63 B.C., and assisted Cicero in suppressing the Catilinarian conspiracy, by capturing the legates of the Allobroges, and procuring from them the evidence which they held in their hands. Two years later he defeated the Allobroges, when they broke out into revolt.

Praeneste, -is, n. and f.: now *Palestrina*, about twenty miles S.E. of Rome, one of the most ancient cities of Latium. According to the legends its origin was Greek. It was strongly fortified by nature and art, and long resisted the attacks of Rome. In 81 B.C. Sulla planted one of his military colonies there. Its oracular temple of Fortune was very celebrated.

R.

Reāte, -is, n.: a town of the Sabines, of which Cicero was the *patronus*. It was before 88 B.C. a *praefectura*, *i.e.* a town governed by a *praefectus* sent from Rome as delegate of the praetor. From 88 B.C. it became, like the other states of Italy, a country town of Roman citizens, but was still called a *praefectura*.

S.

Sāturnīnus, -i, m.: Lucius Appuleius Saturninus, the celebrated demagogue, was tribune of the people for the first time in 102 B.C., and a close adherent of the democratic party of Gaius Marius. In

100 B.C., when Marius was consul and Glaucia praetor, Saturninus by murder and violence contrived to be elected tribune a second time; and he then brought forward various agrarian and other democratic proposals.   In the elections of the year the violent conduct of Saturninus and Glaucia culminated in open assassination, which alienated from them all sympathy.   The senate declared them public enemies; and Marius, as consul, was compelled to act against them.   They took refuge in the Capitol, but were compelled to surrender.   Marius placed them for safety in the Curia; but the mob tore off the roof, and stoned them to death with the tiles.   As long after as the year 63 B.C. Cicero defended the aged senator Rabirius, who was accused of having murdered Saturninus.

Scīpĭo, -ōnis, m.: (1) Publius Cornelius Scipio *Africanus Maior* was born 234 B.C.   He survived the fatal day of Cannae (216 B.C.), where he fought as military tribune and withstood the rash proposal of the young nobles to abandon Italy in despair.   In 210 B.C. he was chosen to command in Spain, though not of the legal age.   In three years he drove the Carthaginians from Spain, and was elected consul for the year 205 B.C.   Crossing into Africa, he at last decisively defeated Hannibal himself in the battle of Zama, 202 B.C., and thus ended the Second Punic war.   For these successes he gained the title Africanus. His great enemy was Cato, called the Censor, who finally triumphed over him and compelled him to retire in disgust from Rome by involving him in the disgrace of his brother Lucius Cornelius Scipio Asiagenes (185 B.C.).   He died about 183 B.C.   (2) Publius Cornelius Scipio *Africanus Minor* was in reality no blood relation of the conqueror of Hannibal, but the adopted son of his eldest son Publius. By birth he was the younger son of Lucius Aemilius Paulus, the conqueror of Macedonia.   Hence after adoption his full name ran P. Corn. Scipio Aemilianus.   He was born about 185 B.C., and when scarcely seventeen fought with distinction at Pydna, where Perseus the last king of Macedon was defeated.   In 146 B.C. he brought the Third Punic War to an end by destroying Carthage; by this success he earned of right his adoptive grandfather's title of Africanus.   In 142 B.C. he was censor, and being elected consul for 134 B.C. he captured Numantia in the following year.   His approval of the murder of Tiberius Gracchus cost him the favour of the people; and in 129 B.C., after a violent scene in the Senate, he was found dead in his bed, the democratic leader Carbo being suspected of his murder. Unlike the elder Africanus, he was severe and simple in his life, and though a lover of Greek literature he was attached to all that was best in the old Roman character.

Servīlĭus, -i, m.: Gaius Servilius Glaucia was praetor in the year 100 B.C.   He was the chief supporter of Saturninus, whose fate he shared.   See Saturninus.

Sestĭus, -i, m.: Publius Sestius (or Sextius) was quaestor in 63 B.C., and tribune of the people six years later.   In 56 B.C. Cicero successfully defended him on a charge of violence. In the civil war he first joined Pompeius, then went over to Caesar. His ultimate fate is unknown.

Sībyllīni lïbri: the original Sibylline books were obtained by Tarquinius Superbus from a Sibyl or wise woman, who is said to have offered nine for sale at first, and, on the king's refusal to purchase them, to have returned with six and then with three, demanding the same price on each occasion. The king purchased the three, and these were kept in the Temple of Jupiter Capitolinus and consulted by special officials called *Decemviri Sacris faciundis*, when prodigies or calamities alarmed the state. When the temple of Jupiter Capitolinus, in the year 83 B.C., was destroyed by fire, these books perished, but their place was supplied by others collected from Italy, Greece, and Asia Minor, by commissioners appointed for the purpose.

Sīlānus, -i, m. : Decimus Junius Silanus was consul designate with Murena in 63 B.C. as a result of the consular elections postponed from October 21st to October 28th. At the meeting of the Senate convened by Cicero on December 5th, to consider the penalty to be inflicted on the Catilinarians, Silanus, as consul elect, was asked for his *sententia* first. He proposed that the prisoners should be put to death, but after the speech of Caesar said that he would agree to the compromise of postponing the discussion.

Stătīlius, -ii, m. : Lucius Statilius was one of the conspirators who was put to death with Lentulus and three others.

Sulla, -ae, m. : Lucius Cornelius Sulla served as quaestor under Marius in Africa (107 B.C.), and under the same general distinguished himself in the conflict with the Cimbri and Teutones. When the Social War broke out (90 B.C.), both Marius and Sulla took an active part against the common foe, but the former was eclipsed by his younger rival, and his jealousy was roused still further when the command in the Mithradatic War was conferred upon Sulla (88 B.C.). After concluding peace with Mithradates, Sulla returned to Italy (83 B.C.), and by the battle of the Colline Gate became master of Rome (82 B.C.). He used his power mercilessly against his political foes, his aim being to extirpate the popular party. He was appointed dictator, and introduced most important changes in the constitution, with the object of restoring the ancient form of government and the authority of the Senate. In the year 79 B.C., to the astonishment of all, he resigned his dictatorship and retired into private life : he died in the next year.

Sulpĭcius, -ii, m. : Publius Sulpicius Rufus, at the outset of his career, was a supporter of the moderate aristocratic party, but, probably bribed by Marius, he suddenly espoused the popular cause, and proposed the law conferring upon Marius the command against Mithradates. When Sulla drove Marius from Rome, Sulpicius was betrayed by a slave near the marshes of Laurentum, and put to death.

T.

Torquātus, -i, m.: Lucius Manlius Torquatus was consul in 65 B.C. with Cotta.

Tullus, -i, m.: Lucius Volcatius Tullus was consul with Lepidus in 66 B.C. See Lepidus.

U.

Umbrēnus, -i, m.: Publius Umbrenus, a man who had formerly carried on business in Gaul, was employed by Lentulus as an agent in bribing the Allobroges.

V.

Vesta, -ae, f.: the goddess of the hearth and the home. Her temple was situated at the south-east corner of the Forum; in it was the holy hearth of the city, the fire on which was kept burning by *Virgines Vestales*, or priestesses of Vesta, who were vowed to a life of chastity.

Volturcius, -ii, m.: a native of Crotona, who was sent by Lentulus to accompany the ambassadors of the Allobroges. Under promise of a free pardon he turned informer.